FOOD AND DRINK IN
ARGENTINA

A Guide For
Tourists and Residents

Dereck Foster
Richard Tripp

AROMAS y
SABORES

El Paso, Texas
Buenos Aires

Aromas y Sabores, El Paso, Texas 79902
www.aromasysabores.com
© 2006 by Aromas y Sabores. All rights reserved.
Protected under the Berne Convention

11 10 09 08 07 06   12 11 10 9 8 7 6 5 4 3 2

Library of Congress Control Number: 2005933362

ISBN 0-9772176-0-4

Acknowledgements
See page 127

Over—A fruit and vegetable stand on Ruta 11 near Arocena,
Santa Fe.

Contents

About This Book

One of the attractions about traveling is the chance to try new foods and drinks. Whatever your tastes you will always hope to find something to catch your eye and satisfy your wants and curiosity. This book is designed to help you fill these expectations by introducing you to the flavors of Argentina.

However, this book is designed to be more than a tourist guide and help that primarily focuses on menus. It is also aimed at those who, for various reasons, have decided to take up residence for shorter or longer periods, and are concerned with buying food for preparation at home. Finding one's way in unfamiliar surroundings, languages and customs can be

Top—Near the end of the Andes, Ushuaia.
Left—Iguazú Falls

traumatic, especially when shopping is involved. This book attempts to solve most of these problems by offering translations of the most common names and terms, with detailed explanations when necessary, with some comparisons between Argentine, U.S. and European customs, usages and techniques. Deciding what to include has not been easy. Spain and Italy are the dominant culinary influences but it is beyond the scope of this book to include all of the Spanish and Italian terms one might encounter.

While this is not a cookbook, a number of typical or unusual recipes have been included to illustrate aspects of local cuisine, and to help you recreate the memories of your travels once back home.

As is common to the world at large, basic foods

are universal. Rice, potatoes, tomatoes, maize (corn) and many other staples are found worldwide but are handled in quite contrasting ways. Argentina can be classified—in its true, native cuisine—as a land of maize and beef, which joined with the indigenous potato forms an almost unbeatable trio. However, there is a large gap between the cuisine of the big cities and the regional food of the common, mostly rural or semi-rural, population. One aim of this book is to highlight some of these differences.

In addition to all this, a short glossary of *"lunfardo"* (Buenos Aires slang) has been included as these terms will often crop up when in contact with local tradesmen. No attempt has been made to do the same with slang for other regions, such as Misiones and Corrientes, where

Guaraní terms are often incorporated.

British English terms are used throughout with American English terms added as needed for clarity.

It is beyond the scope of this guide to provide more than a short list of the most reliable restaurants in Buenos Aires plus a few in other cities. In the case of wines—a major Argentine product—the list is also reduced to the most reliable bodegas.

A Last Word: Are the people called Argentines or Argentineans? The natives of Argentina who speak English prefer Argentine, with a certain logic. In English, Argentina is more formally called The Republic of Argentina or The Argentine Republic. It is logical therefore, to use "Argentine" as the distinctive adjective.

One of the many icebergs floating on Lago Argentino.

Food of Argentina

Food of Argentina

Culinary History

Argentina forms part of South America, and is a former Spanish colony. More than any other South American nation, it has best preserved a definitely European culture (in spite of strong North American influence that commenced around the 1960s.)

When the first Spanish explorers arrived, they found a large, mostly fertile region almost totally devoid of any natural produce other than abundant bird life and small animals, such as *guanacos*, *ñandú* (a type of ostrich), and *huemules* (a local member of the deer family). The natives lived mainly off guanacos when desirous of meat.

Only in the remote northeast and northwest corners were the influences of the Guaraní tribes and Incas, respectively, to be found. The Spaniards introduced cattle, horses, poultry and vegetables, while adopting the potato (a South American vegetable) and largely rejecting maize *(corn)* (another South American citizen). As a result, Argentine cooking is based largely on European approaches and tradition. A truly national or local cuisine is hard to find and

Left—Dining room of a small inn in Colon, Entre Rios. Preceeding—Street parrilla in Belgrano, Buenos Aires.

The back of a gaucho dressed for the *feria* at Mataderos.

what little there is, is based on maize related combinations, an Inca inheritance. (For some reason, the Spaniards largely rejected this versatile food, and even today such common delights as "*corn on the cob*" are shunned in Spain as being food for pigs.)

The Spanish tradition lingered on until Spanish America began to throw off the Spanish yoke and fresh European airs began to blow away Hispanic cobwebs. These airs came mainly from France. In Argentina, for the top social strata—there were only two, the other being the lower classes—France (particularly Paris) was the country and culture to imitate. Later, starting around 1880 and lasting until the 1930s, Argentina experienced an important wave of European immigrants. While most were Spanish and Italian, a large minority included other Europeans, both East and West, and many from the Middle East. Today the cuisine of Buenos Aires, in particular, and other large cities reflects a venerable mix of culinary influences from both the West and (recently) the East. However, Spanish and Italian cooking dominates.

One result of the mixture of cultures is a linguistic fusion of food terms from various languages with the result that the words for many ingredients and preparations are different from those elsewhere in Latin America or Spain.

Impact of Economic and Cultural Factors

Although Argentina is a major producer of agricultural products, as a result of economic and cultural factors only small quantities of some

Below—Hotel Llao Llao, Bariloche, Rio Negro seen from lake Nahuel Huapi.

Ruins of the Jesuit Mission of San Ignacio, Misiones.

products are available in its internal markets, the bulk having been exported. Some examples:

Large European hares run wild in Patagonia, having been introduced many years ago. Many are captured, killed and processed for export to Europe, but it is almost impossible to find them in an Argentine *carniceria* or featured on a restaurant menu, even in Patagonia.

In 2002, Argentina was the world's largest exporter of honey. Much of its production was sold in Europe at a premium due to its quality and organic nature, and because it could be differentiated by floral source. At the same time, at the Argentine Honey producer's cooperative store in Buenos Aires, the honey was only differentiated by the province from which it came.

The fine Catamarcan *aguardiente* that commands a premium price in Europe is difficult to find in Argentina except in Catamarca from vendors of artesanal products.

Despite the wealth and size of Buenos Aires, there are no gourmet stores. It has nothing comparable to Robs of Brussels, Fouchon of Paris, Fortnam & Mason of London, Dean & DeLuca of New York, or even the gourmet section of El Corte Inglés of Madrid.

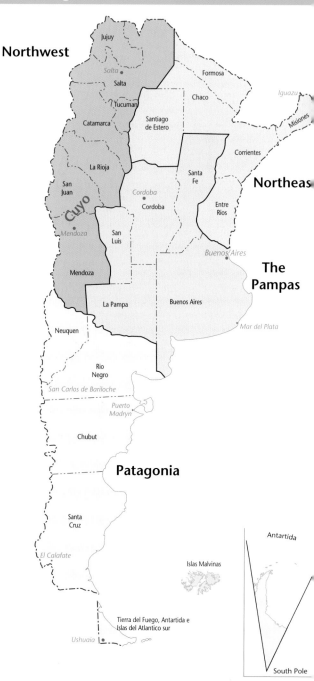

Northwest

Jujuy

Salta

Salta

Tucuman

Catamarca

Santiago
de Estero

Formosa

Chaco

Iguazu

Misiones

Corrientes

Northeas

La Rioja

San
Juan

Cuyo

Cordoba

Cordoba

Santa
Fe

Entre
Rios

Mendoza

San
Luis

Buenos Aires

The
Pampas

Mendoza

La Pampa

Buenos Aires

Mar del Plata

Neuquen

Rio
Negro

San Carlos de Bariloche

Puerto
Madryn

Chubut

Patagonia

Santa
Cruz

El Calafate

Antartida

Islas Malvinas

Tierra del Fuego, Antartida e
Islas del Atlantico sur

Ushuaia

South Pole

The Main Food Regions

For gastronomic purposes, Argentina can be divided into four main regions (including two sub-regions). These are: The Pampas, Northwest (with Cuyo), Northeast or Littoral (with Entre Rios), and Patagonia. Within these regions, there are areas of influence such as the Welsh in a corner of Patagonia, the Swedish in a part of Misiones, and German and central European influences in the Lake Districts of Patagonia and portions of Cordoba.

The Pampas Home of the gaucho and the pampas indians, both nomadic by nature, this is the home of the basic foods: roast meats and little else. Only in the cities and settlements did a more organized cuisine evolve, based largely on beef, using the huge free-roaming herds as their source of supply. Thus were conceived a number of derivative foods such as the puchero, stews, sausages, cold cuts and dairy products such as cheese and milk puddings.

Greater Buenos Aires, including the Capital Federal, with 38% of Argentina's some 36 million inhabitants, exerts a strong influence on the culture and gastronomy of the country. Throughout its history, Buenos Aires has been Argentina's principal seaport and point of entry for immigrants with their ideas of gastronomy which then unevenly worked their way across the country. With open immigration after independence, European (mostly Italian) influences began to be felt, particu-

Top—An orchard in the Province of San Juan.

Looking toward Aconcagua, the highest mountain outside of the Himalayas, with its peak hidden in the clouds.

larly that of pastas and pizzas.

Northwest Touching the borders with Chile and Bolivia, and comprising the provinces of Salta, Jujuy, Catamarca and La Rioja, the Northwest is the center of what remains of Inca influence still found in Argentine cuisine. This is the kingdom of maize and all of its derivatives even though maize is principally harvested in the pampas. *Humitas*, *patascas*, *locros*, and similar are examples of the cuisine. Further south in the area known as Cuyo, covering the provinces of San Juan and Mendoza, the Inca influence has been softened by the effects of the proximity of the pampas.

The cheeses made in the Tafi valley of Tucumán are celebrated but hard to obtain because their production is limited. The lemons and sugar cane of Tucumán are proverbial. Tucumán is also a stronghold of the alfajor and marzipan. Argentine marzipan is different from the Spanish version because Argentine marzipan uses wheat flour instead of ground almonds. Catamarca is the home of excellent *aguardiente* (See page 67) while Salta, La Rioja, San Juan and Mendoza are important wine areas; discussed in "Wine & Drink of Argentina" on page 55.

Northeast The Northeast, also called Mesopotamia or Litoral, with its center based on the provinces of Misiones and Corrientes, is strongly marked by Guaraní cuisine (and that of Southwest Brazil). Farina, manioc flour and the root of the iñame form the tripod upon which this cuisine is based. Even today, in this area manioc flour is more widely used than wheat flour, although it is not unusual for a mixture of manioc and white maize flour *(corn meal)* to be used. The foods are completely local and can only be found by visiting the region (and then not everywhere). The southeast of this area, comprising the province of Entre Rios, especially the south, is more inclined toward the pampas style of eating. The production of yerba mate is very important economically for this area and its consumption as mate is important in the daily life and culture of the region.

A table set for a traditional Welsh Tea in Gaiman.

Patagonia Today this vast semi-arid region is known as the home of some of the world's best lamb. Its vast coast is only now being exploited to any extent, with oysters, mussels and the celebrated Fuegian Spider (or King) Crab leading the way. In the Andean valleys fruits and berries are a backbone of the local economy, with mushrooms, trout and game in second place. A certain foreign flavor is to be found in some areas, such as the Welsh colony in Gaiman (province of Chubut) and

A boatload of tourists putting out to sea to watch whales at Puerto Pirámides, Peninsula Valdes, Chubut.

15

A customer selecting cheese at a Tandil cheese store.

its surroundings and a Germanic influence in Bariloche and further south, following the Andean foothills, These same foothills are a great source of a varied number of mushrooms only now being slowly recognized as a commercial asset and exploited. This region is also a source of fine wines, which are discussed in "Wine & Drink of Argentina" on page 55.

Characteristic Dishes

Cooking Techniques

Argentine cuisine, like so many others, is largely based on a relatively small number of repetitive dishes. *Fiambres* (cold cuts), *asados* (roasts of many types), *bifes* (steaks), and *flan* (baked custards) are but a few of the items that appear on most normal—as opposed to sophisticated—menus. In large and medium cities the hamburger has carved out an important niche.

The Argentine cooking style might be considered minimalist. Meat is generally grilled or roasted with only salt and pepper. Marinades are simple and light, nothing like a U.S. barbecue sauce. Other than fried potatoes and squid, little food is deep fried, sautéing being the preferred method for seafood. Except for cumin, the seasonings used with vegetables and meats are herbs rather than spices, with a limited set even then: oregano, basil, thyme, rosemary, bay leaf. Very few dishes are spicy hot. Even the food in Thai restaurants has been modified to be less spicy to suit Argentine taste buds. Following are some examples of what to expect on an Argentine table. Even if you are not planning to do any cooking, a quick glance through the recipes starting on page 103 should also improve your feel for Argentine cooking techniques.

Alfajor Like many foods whose Spanish name begins with "al," Argentina's *alfajor* has an Arabic origin. An *alfajor* consists of two round tablets of pastry—whose texture and preparation vary regionally— joined together by a sweet filling. By far the most traditional filling is *dulce de leche*. Bathed in either a sugar or chocolate coating, they are obtainable almost anywhere food is sold. They are well worth sampling. Although in the city and province of Buenos Aires, *alfajores* of other regions (Cordoba, Santa Fe, Mar de Plata and others) are widely available, this is not necessarily the case in other regions where local alfajores dominate the market.

Cheeses Argentina is an important exporter of industrially produced cheeses, especially of the Italian style which are sold as that type of cheese, e.g., mozzarella. However, some of the leading cheese encyclopedias of today identify at least nine cheeses as being Argentine. They are as follows:

Atuel—Closely resembles Port Salut. Semi–firm, milky and mild.

Cafayate—A cheese very similar to the Tafí, developed in the area adjacent to the Tafí Valley.

Chubut—Semi–firm, mild, slightly peppery

17

when mature. Despite the name, it has no connection with the province.

Cuartirolo—This is an Argentine version of the Italian Lombard cheese "Quartirolo." Soft, sweet and fast ripening.

Artesanal cheeses aging in a Tandil dairy.

Goya—This cheese from Corrientes is very hard to find. It is a grating cheese similar to an Asiago. Peppery and highly flavoured.

Huemul—This is almost totally forgotten and unavailable. Semi–firm, mildly herbal.

Provoleta—This is a version of Provolone. Light yellow to golden brown, firm-textured with a mild, sometimes sharp flavor; melts quickly when shredded.

Tafí—This cheese resulted from the efforts of the early Spanish settlers of the Tafí Valley to imitate the Spanish Manchego. Different herbs

and cows ensured an original and characteristic flavour. Semi–firm, rightly piquant.

Tandil—Danish settlers close to the city of Tandil created this cheese, similar to a Cantal. Tastes slightly of salt, and slightly of mountain herbs.

Dulce de leche It is hard to go anywhere in Argentina and not be confronted at some stage by this creamy, almost over–sweet milk confection. In desserts, bakery products, confectionery and as a flavoring, dulce de leche is an Argentine passion. It is not however, an Argentine creation, despite many people's belief. It is a member of the family of foods grouped under the generic name of caramel and more specifically, toffee. A result of the so-called "Streckeo degradation"—when sugar is heated in milk, it reacts with the milk proteins—it is found in slightly differing versions in Chile (*Manjar blanco*), Colombia (*Arequipe*), Mexico (*Cajeta de celaya*), and Paraguay and Ecuador.

Empanada Eating was easy in the beginning. Food was raw and was

there for the taking. Then along came fire and cooked hot food made its bow, long before the creation of the spoon or fork. Fingers were used and the problem was how to keep them from being burned. Wrapping hot food in some sort of protection was the answer.

Empanadas, in concept if not name, must certainly be one of the earliest forms of finger food. Originally the wrapping was a piece of bread but with the passing of time special doughs were created, enabling the creation of little (or not so little) packets. Empanada literally means "coated in bread," a description that covers a multitude of forms, from a "weiner-schnitzel" to "Scotch Eggs." However, an Argentine empanada does not fit into this category but into that best described by the generic terms of pasty and turnovers.

To make them, a thin sheet of round dough has some filling placed on it and the dough is folded over, forming a packet which is then baked or fried—a concept similar to ravioli, which are boiled.

A true (traditional) beef empanada has its beef finely chopped by hand, thus avoiding the loss of juice and moisture that occurs when meat is mechanically ground. Leaving aside the actual filling, of which there are very many kinds and variations, empanadas are distinguished by their regional origin.

Almost all of Argentina's provinces boast of "their" empanada, reflecting regional preferences for the degree of spiciness, the selection of different condimenting ingredients (olives, raisins, pimiento, potato, etc.) and the means of cooking: baking or frying. The most widely recognized styles are: Catamarca, Salta, Jujuy, and Tucumán. Famaillá, a village in Tucumán, is known for its chicken-based empanada. There are also several non-region-specific ones incorporating seafood, such as fish, or shrimp. Another non-region-specific type is the Arab empanada. (In Argentina "Arab" is used in a non-derogatory manner to refer to people of Middle

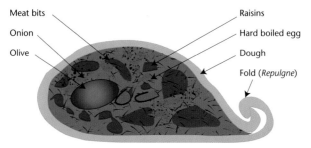

Meat bits
Onion
Olive
Raisins
Hard boiled egg
Dough
Fold (*Repulgne*)

Cross section of an empanada

Eastern origin, lumping together Lebanese, Syrians, Palestinians, etc.)

The fold or *"repulgue"* of the empananda is marked in some way to let patrons know what it is filled with but these markings are not consistent from place to place.

There is a special etiquette for eating empanadas:

a) Fingers are used rather than a fork.

b) Hold the empanada by one tip and bite the other. This allows steam to escape if the empanada is very hot, and prevents a burnt lip or tongue.

c) Wrap a napkin around your wrist if the empanada is of the juicy kind (those from Salta, for example) to avoid hot liquid from running out and causing burns or stains that are hard to remove.

For some reason, empanadas seem to taste better when eaten standing up and out of doors.

A beef empanada and a good glass of red wine is an unbeatable combination.

Escabeche A marinade of oil, vinegar and herbs used in olden times to preserve meat and vegetables. Today it is used as a means of giving flavor and tenderizing. Many local products can be found preserved in escabeche at artesanal markets throughout Argentina. See "Escabeche" on page 105.

Humita This is an indegenous preparation of freshly grated corn kernels wrapped in *chala* (corn leaves) and boiled, similar to a corn flour dumpling. Humitas are the ancestors of the tamale. This creamy preparation can be sweet or savory. The latter version is more popular in

Buenos Aires and environs, the former in the Northwest. In some regions, mashed *zapallo* is added to the mixture.

Locro This is a thick soup or stew. There are many regional variations and recipes are elastic. Basically, a locro is a dish of hominy which is stewed with a wide selection of ingredients which could include beef, bacon, knuckle bones, onion, tomato, squash, potato, sweet potato, and spring onion, condimented with paprika, cumin, oregano, red hot pepper and bay leaf. Sausages, pork trotters and beans are also popular but rarely chicken and never fish.

Milanesa One of the most popular meat dishes in Argentina is a Milanesa, consisting of a thin cut of beef, which is breaded and fried. It will appear on almost every menu and is something common in most homes. In a restaurant it is usually accompanied by a salad and fried or mashed potatoes.

Panqueque de manzana
This dessert, a local creation, is outstanding when well prepared. Butter and

Locro

sugar are placed in a pan and the butter is heated to melt. A thin covering of batter is introduced and covered with thin slices of apple. When the sugar starts to caramelize, one either (a) flips the *panqueque* over into another pan with butter and sugar already well heated and caramelized, or (b) sugar is sprinkled onto the *panqueque* and then placed under a hot grill until the sugar turns brown. Sabot (see page 83) prepares possibly the best in Buenos Aires.

Revuelto Gramajo
Another Argentine creation that is outstanding when prepared correctly. To prepare it, eggs are slightly scrambled in the pan while cooking slowly in butter. In the final stage, small amounts of chopped ham and chopped chicken breast and very thin matchstick potatoes are added. It is served hot and slightly moist over toasted bread. Very few restaurants include the chicken.

Antique siphon bottles on sale at the market in Plaza Dorrego, San Telmo, Buenos Aires.

A-Z Guide to Argentine Foods

Key to Authors' Ratings

Normal
✔Worth a try
★Something special

A

A la ..., al ... Indicates the style of preparation. In this guide, such terms are listed according to the style. For example, see "Cruz, a la" on page 31.

Abadejo Pollack, Pink cuskeel. A less flavorful fish than hake (*Merluza*) but cooked the same.

Aderezo A general term for a dressing, such as *salsa golf*.

Adobo A general term for a style of marinade that is sometimes dry and rubbed on meat before cooking. More liquid versions are used to tenderize and flavor meat, fish, or vegetables by marinating for some hours or days. *Also see page 105.*

Aceite Oil

... de Olivas Olive oil

... de maíz Corn oil

Aceitunas Olives

Acelgas Swiss chard

Acerola The fruit of a tree found in the high Paraná river basin. Sometimes called the cherry of the Antilles, it is very high in vitamin C.

Achicoria Chicory

Achuras The general term used for the viscera or offal of cattle, sheep, pork, and goats. It encompasses the heart, liver, small and large intestines, thymus, kidney, testicles, and stomach.

Agridulce Sweet-sour. Used in reference to many preparations from pickles to sauces to empanadas, where an acid or sour flavor is paired with a sweet component.

Ahumado Smoked. Bariloche and Mendoza are

well-known sources of smoked cheeses, duck, pheasant, trout, salmon, venison, and wild boar.

Ajedrea Savory (the herb).

Ají General term for peppers.

Ajillo, al Cooked in a garlic sauce.

Ajo Garlic

Albahaca Basil

Albóndigas Dumplings if associated with a vegetable (*albóndigas de acelgas*); otherwise meatballs (of beef if unstated). In Argentina the basic technique has been adopted to use indigenous materials such as river fish and ñandú.

Alcaparra Caper

Alcaucil Artichoke

Alcayota See "Cayote" on page 27.

✓ **Alfajor** Sandwich biscuit (*cookie*). See page 17.

Alfeñiques Also known as *melcocha*, these candies of Arab-Spanish origin are especially popular in the Puna. Made of honey or cane syrup cooked to the desired consistency when they are formed or molded into shapes, often human figures.

Aliñado Similar to an *adobo*, an aliñado is an uncooked dressing or marinade used to dress or flavor roasted or grilled meats and vegetables, including salads.

Almendra Almond. A dish prepared *almendrado* will be coated with almonds.

Almíbar, en In syrup

Alubia White beans

Ambrosía A fruit-flavored egg custard. A favorite dessert of the revered President Sarmiento from whom the name came because he called it "ambrosia."

Ananá Pineapple. *Ananá* is the Guaraní name for the fruit. Named *piña* by the Spanish when they arrived because it reminded them of the pinecones in Spain, thus providing the basis for its English form.

Ananás Variety of melon

Anchoa Anchovy

Anchi A popular, very sweet dessert of the Northwest, consisting of a thick creamy mixture of corn flour (*corn meal*), orange or lemon juice and raisins.

Ancua Toasted corn. Of Quechua origin, *ancua* refers to large grains of corn that have been toasted. Term used in the Cuyo. In the northeast, *flor de ancua* is used to refer to popcorn. See "Pochoclo" on page 48.

Anguila Eel. The *anguila criolla* is a true native of Argentina and unlike the European eels, does not spend part of its life cycle in the ocean. Delicious, especially when smoked.

Antojo Whim, craving; a catch-all term sometimes used to indicate specialty food items.

Apanado Breaded

Aperitivo Aperitif when referring to a drink, otherwise snack or appetizer.

Apio Celery

Arándano Blueberry

Armado The common name given to certain members of the *bagres* family, a fish caught in the River Plate basin, prized for its meat, and important economically.

Arrope Inherited from the ancient Inca culture, *arropes* are fairly thick syrups obtained by boiling the sap of various trees, e.g., *chañar*, or fruits such as that of the cactus, *tuna*. The name also applies to syrups obtained from other fruit such as the grape, plum and apricot. A popular dessert, in Salta and the north in particular, is *"quesillo de cabra con arrope,"* a mild flavored white goat cheese with *tuna arrope*.

Arroz Rice or rice dishes.

Arroz de vigilia Lenten rice

✔ **Arroz con Leche** A creamy rice pudding, served cold, lightly flavored with lemon, usually dusted with cinnamon.

Artesanal Handcrafted, prepared using traditional methods. (e.g., *"Quesos artesanal"* indicates farm-house cheeses.)

Arveja Peas

Atún Tuna. The species caught in Argentine waters are: Albacore, Yellow Fin, Southern Bluefin and Big Eye. The Bluefin and the Bigeye tunas are recognized by their reddish colored steaks. Their smaller relatives, the Yellow Fin and Albacore tuna have lighter colored steaks. Properly cooked tuna has a firm consistency, almost like a pork chop, and is firmer than the familiar canned tuna.

Avati A term used in the Northwest for maize.

Azúcar Sugar

... blanco/común White sugar

... impalpable Icing sugar

... moreno Brown sugar

B

Bacalao (Austral) Southern Cod. A classic white fish with a pleasingly mild taste and a semi-firm flesh.

Bagna cauda A hot garlic-anchovy sauce used for dipping bread and vegetables. Brought to the Santa Fe area by Italian immigrants from the Piedmont.

Bagre A species of freshwater catfish widely distributed in the bays, rivers and lakes of Argentina. With an oily flesh, it is considered good eating. Its members include the armado.

Baguette Long thin loaf of bread.

Balancho A paste made from *mistol* (a fruit from a wild bush of the same name) coated with flour and dried in the sun.

Banana Banana

Batatas

✓**Batata** Yam. Off white or brown skin and white, light yellow or pink flesh. Although often referred to as sweet potato, it is not as sweet as the sweet potato.

Berenjena Eggplant, aubergine.

Berros Watercress

Besugo Bream (Red) or Red porgy (Pagrus Pagrus). Has a delicious lean and flaky flesh but is bony.

Bife A lean cut of beef taken from various parts of the animal. The most common being *bife de costilla, de chorizo, de lomo,* and *de cuadril.*

✓**... de chorizo** A thick boneless steak, similar to a New York Strip steak. Sometimes offered *"mariposa"* or butterflied, where it is split in half before cooking.

... de costilla T-Bone steak

... de lomo Loin steak

Bifes Cordobeses Boneless steaks of young beef, breaded, lightly fried, coated in beaten egg and then fried again.

Bifes a la Criolla Steaks slowly cooked in a casserole with oil, onions, sliced potatoes, tomatoes, peppers, garlic and parsley.

Bifes a la Portuguesa Steaks seasoned with salt and pepper, sauteed over a slow fire in oil, to which is then added onions and sweet peppers previously cooked in butter.

Blanco White, as in *vino blanco.* Also used to indicate white or breast meat, such as *blanco de pavo.*

★**Boga** A fresh-water fish found in the feeder rivers of the River Plate, it is prevalent near the grain docks, where it feeds on the grain that falls into the water during the loading process. Excellent flavor and texture.

Bolanchao Small baked balls of mistol. (See Balancho).

Bolas de fraile Fried balls of yeast-risen dough lightly dusted in sugar, of German origin, in Argentina generally filled with dulce de leche. Literally translated *Monks Balls,* the name is believed to come from their resemblance to the tassels on the cords binding the robes worn by some monks.

Bolitos de anise Small sweet anise flavored biscuits, of Arab origin, that are generally eaten while drinking mate, especially in Tucumán and Santiago del Estero.

Bonito A variety of tuna.

Bróculi Broccoli

Brotes Sprouts, *brotes de soja.*

Brótola The Argentine fish *brótola,* (*urophicis brasiliensis*) or Brazilian

Codling is sometimes confused with the *brótola de roca*, (*Phycis phycis*). Both have a white mild flavored flaky flesh when cooked.

Budín Pudding, loaf cake, or pie. The very loosely used term is applied to such a diverse set of preparations as *budín inglés, budín chocolate, budín de pan, budín de alcauciles,* and *budín de choclo*.

★**Budín de choclo** Corn pudding. See "Budín de Choclo al Caramelo" on page 108.

Buñuelos Fried puffs. Made from flour or mashed potatoes. Can be sweet or savory, depending on other ingredients. The savory versions are generally called *croquetas*.

Buseca A dish of Italian origin using tripe and vegetables in a tomato sauce, related to a *guiso de mondongo*.

Butifarra A white fresh pork sausage; originally from Catalunya.

C

Caballa Mackerel, this fish's flesh is fatty, rich-flavored, moist, and is often cooked with acidic flavorings such as lemon or tomato.

Caballo, a "On horseback," such as *bife de chorizo a caballo,* a preparation that means it will be served topped with a fried egg.

Cabra Goat. There are several regions in Argentina, particularly the Cuyo, in which the goat is more common than cattle and its meat, *chivito*, appears on menus at least as often as beef.

Caburé A cake resembling the chipá.

Calabaza In Argentina this is generally used to refer to only one type of squash, the anco. See "Zapallo" on page 53.

Calafate Blue, intensely flavored berries from a thorny Patagonian bush, used in jellies, preserves, ice cream, and liqueurs. Two different plants with similar fruit share the common name. Although some consider the plant a type of "barberry", it is unique to Chile and Argentina.

Calamar Squid, several different varieties sold.

Calamarete Small squid, usually served fried whole.

Caldo Broth

Caldillo Vegetables cooked in a meat broth; something closer to a stew than a soup.

Camarón Shrimp

Canela Cinnamon

Cangrejo rojo Deep sea red crab

Caipirinha The name for a popular Brazilian drink, it is often displayed in markets identifying the limes used to make the drink. See page 67.

Caquís Small red fruit from a tree of Japanese origin with mild sweet pulp,

Carbonada

used in jellies and preserves.

Caracoles General term for sea snails such as whelks.

✓**Carbonada** A stew originating in Chile, Perú and the region of the River Plate. Contains beef, corn on the cob, pumpkin, vegetables, sugar, vinegar, raisins, peaches (in season), and a few regional touches.

Cardamomo Cardamom.

Carne Meat

Carne vacuna Beef

✓**Carne cortada a cuchillo** Meat which has been cut by knife. Used in reference to the meat in empanadas to indicate that it is not ground meat (hamburger meat).

Carpaccio Very thinly sliced rare roast beef dressed with lemon juice, olive oil and capers. Usage of term has been expanded to include other very thinly sliced food items, such as salmon, marrows (zucchini), and aubergines (egg plants).

Carpincho The largest rodent in the world, it resembles a deer in appearance. Widely established in the Northeast and wet pampas, it is hunted for its savory meat and skin.

★**Carre ahumado** Smoked pork loin.

Cáscara The outer covering or skin; meaning rind of citrus fruits, shells of nuts and skin of potatoes.

Casera Home-made. This term is never used on commercially prepared products. Thus, for example, *flan casera* indicates it was made on premises.

✓**Cayote** Fig leaf gourd, usually found as *dulce de cayote*, pieces in sugar syrup.

Cazón Variety of shark; a shellfish eater, it is reputed for its excellent flavor.

Cazuela Casserole.

Cazuela Argentina A stew of chickpeas, chicken, corn (maize), vegetables and rice.

Cebiche See "Seviche" on page 51.

Cebolla Onion

Cebolla de verdeo Spring onion.

Cebolleta verde Scallion, small green onion.

Cebollino Chive

Cebollito Chive

★**Centolla** Snow crab, southern king crab. While there are several excellent preparations, a serving of plain centolla cannot be surpassed.

Centollon Spider crab

Cereza Cherry. Eaten fresh or used in pies and other desserts.

Ceviche See "Seviche" on page 51.

A live centolla being displayed on a tour boat in Ushuaia.

Champiñón Common white mushroom.

Champiñón marrón Common brown mushroom.

Chanfaina A type of stew incorporating onions, tomatoes and peppers and usually hearts and livers, normally of goats or lamb with regional variations. There is a Patagonian version made with fish.

Charqui Also written *"charque,"* this dried beef is the local version of the South African biltong, the Italian bresaola and the jerky of the U.S. Found mainly in the Northeast, the most usual way it is eaten is as a *charquicán.* A traditional pre-Colombian Peruvian and Bolivian preparation.

Charquicán A stew which includes onions, vegetable marrows *(zucchinis),* carrots, potatoes, garlic and a medley of herbs. It is claimed that the best charqui and charquicán is to be found in Salta. If encountered in a restaurant outside of the Northwest, it is probably prepared using fresh meat rather than charqui.

Chatre Flat hollow baked biscuits *(cookies),* usually dusted with sugar or spread with dulce de leche.

Chaucha de vainilla Vanilla bean

Chauchas Green beans (used by itself it usually means flat green beans).

Chauchas rollizas String beans.

Chaya A typical stew of the Patagonia made of ñandú or guanaco.

Chernia Stone Bass. Mediterranean Sea Bass; a flaky and relatively firm textured fish that has a mild but distinctive flavor that is highly prized.

Chicharrón Small bits of crisp fat left over after rendering pork or beef fat. Sometimes used as a flavoring ingredient in *pan de campo, tortas* and *bizcochos.*

Chichoca Slices of fruit or vegetables dried in the sun. In the North peppers, tomatoes, egg plants and squashes are dried in this manner.

Chico/a Small. A frequently encountered term, in such queries as whether you want *"un chico,"* small portion or *un grande*, large one.

★**Chimichurri** An Argentine marinade, also used as a dressing or salsa for grilled meats. Recipes vary widely, some being more piquant than others. See recipe on page 106.

Chinchulínes The second portion of the small intestine of beef. A common component of an asado.

Chipás.

Chipá The bread of Paraguay and the provinces of Corrientes and Misiones. Made with manioc flour, corn flour, egg, fat, and almost always cheese.

Chipá-guazú A casserole of grated corn, fat, and milk, well mixed and baked.

Chirimoya The *Chirimoya* or Custard Apple is a strange looking fruit, with a light green, scaly looking exterior that conceals a lusciously sweet pulp best eaten with a spoon; its large black seeds are easily discarded.

Chistorra A lean, slightly smoked link pork sausage colored and flavored with sweet paprika; of Basque origin.

Chivito The meat of a young goat; with a bone structure similar to a lamb, both are normally cooked the same way. However, *chivitos* have less fat and are often not as tender. — In areas close to the border with Uruguay, *"Chivito"* may refer to a sandwich similar to a lomito, consisting of a thin slice of meat, with lettuce and tomato between halves of a large roll.

Choclo Corn

Choclo troceado Corn on the cob cut into small pieces. This is a common form of adding corn to dishes.

Choclo desgranado Corn cut from the cob.

Choique Small ñandú. Found in the steppes of Patagonia and in the high Andes plains up to 4000 meters.

★**Choripan** The Argentine version of a sausage in a roll, consisting of a chorizo, generally sliced in half, placed in a crusty roll of appropriate size, normally dressed with chimichurri or mustard, although some add lettuce and tomato. Vendors selling choripan can be found in parks and near football stadiums, popular events and festivals.

Chorizo A thick fresh link sausage containing pork and beef. Argentine chori-

Choripan

zos are very different from those of the same name encountered in Spain or Mexico. They have very few herbs or spices.

Choro Chilean term for mussels. Sometimes found on menus in Patagonia.

Chuchoca Corn kernels dried in the oven or on heated stones and then used in cooking such dishes as locro in the Northwest.

Chulas Marinated steaks with sauce.

Chuño Potato flour made from the naturally freeze dried potatoes (*chumo*)of the frozen high Andes. The technique predates the Incas. The potatoes and the flour are sold in the Northwest and in some markets in Buenos Aires.

Chupe A thick soup of Peruvian origins with many variations but is basically made with meat and vegetables on hand; can contain rice or potatoes.

Chupín A thick fish or shellfish stew common in the Northeast. Made with pieces of river fish, such as Boga and Dorado, common in the River Paraná or River Uruguay, and onion,

tomatoes, red wine and fresh herbs.

Churrasco A boneless steak, usually of cheap beef, usually one or two inches thick.

Churros A type of breakfast fritter of dough extruded into hot fat or oil. Although based upon those popular in Spain, the Argentine version commonly encountered today is straight, fatter and invariably filled with dulce de leche. Normally eaten with mate or hot chocolate.

Ciboulette Chive

Ciruelo Plum.

Clara (de huevo) Egg white.

Clara a nieve Beaten egg whites.

Cochinillo Suckling pig. While both are suckling, a *cochinillo* is younger than a *lechón*.

Codorniz Quail

Cogollos Hearts of lettuce.

Colación A traditional sweet of the Cuyo and Cordoba. It consists of a oval concave biscuit, filled with dulce de leche, and then covered with a bath of white sugar.

Coliflor Cauliflower

Comelotodo Snow pea

Come-todo Snow pea

Comino Cumin. A popular flavoring ingredient for Northwestern Argentine cooking.

Completo Full (breakfast or sandwich) with ham and cheese, maybe boiled egg, added to the ordinary ingredients.

Congrio Conger eel. A semi-fatty fish with a firm, flavorful flesh.

Copetín Aperitif; drinks served before a meal.

Cordero Lamb

Cordero patigonico Lamb from Patagonia. Because it feeds on arid pasture land, it contains little fat. In a *parilla*, this always means roasted "a la cruz." Traditionally, such are cooked for up to five hours. Also outstanding are *"guisos"* of *"cordero patigonico."*

Coriandro Cilantro

Corintos Currants

Cornalito Silverside, a small fish similar to smelt.

Corvina A very flavorful sea fish with a flaky white flesh, similar to a perch or drum. There are two common varieties, *Corvina Negra* and *Corvina Rubia*. The flesh of corvina is white, sweet, lean and finely textured.

Costillar The name given to the entire rib section of a side of meat. Depending on the size and type of animal, it may be cut into small pieces for cooking. *Costillas* refers to a portion cut from the *costillar*.

Crema Cream or a creamy soup. A dish followed by "a *la crema*" indicates a creamy sauce.

Criadillas Testicles of a young bull. A traditional part of an asado in the country, they have a soft flavor similar to a sweetbread. They are scarce,

expensive and seldom encountered in restaurants.

Criollo/a, a la In the creole style, meaning in the old colonial style. In general this means cooked with, or served with, a sauce of onions, sweet peppers, tomatoes, garlic and parsley.

Croquetas Croquettes. The most common are those of chard, spinach, fish and rice. Seldom served as a main dish. Argentine croquettes are always mild flavored, well browned and served without sauce.

Cordero being roasted a la cruz.

Cruz, a la On a cross; used for meat cooked on a vertical spit where the meat is held open by a cross bar so that the spit looks like a cross.

Cuaresmillo Variety of late peach, usually served as dulce de cuaresmillo.

Cuajada A mild, very fresh white cheese; junket; curd.

Cubanitos A sweet consisting of a small tube of sweet, dry, crisp thin pastry, similar to that used in ice cream cones, filled with dulce de leche. Frequently sold by walking venders at fairs, in plazas, and street intersections.

Cuchi A suckling pig, prepared *a adobo* and roasted whole in a brick oven. A traditional dish for certain holidays in the Northeast, such as 25 July, the Day of Saint James. See "Lechón adobado" on page 37.

Cucurucho Ice cream cone.

Curanto A form of indigenous cooking. A pit is dug and small pieces of wood are laid down and topped with flat stones. The wood is burned to coals which are removed, leaving the hot stones. The stones are then covered with leaves of *nalca* or *maqui*, then meat and vegetables, covered with more leaves, a piece of cloth and dirt and left to rest until the food is cooked.

Cuis A type of guinea pig. Once raised by every Inca household for food much as chickens were in Europe. Nowadays seldom to be found on a menu or in the market.

D

Damascos Apricot

Delicias Delights. often used in *confitería* menus as a category to group small sweet items.

A simple breakfast of coffee with medialunas.

Desayuno Breakfast. Most Argentines eat a simple breakfast of coffee or mate with small pastries, toast or yogurt.

Descremado/a Decreamed, milk fat removed. Commonly found on containers of dairy products such as milk, yogurt, cream, and ice cream.

Deshuesado Deboned

Diente de león Dandelion

Disco, al or Disco de Arajo A cooking technique in which meats are cooked by placing them on a hot piece of metal similar to a plowing disc.

Don Pedro An ice cream dessert where scoops of ice cream in a deep glass are washed with whiskey and topped with whipped cream. *Warning*: all too frequently the whiskey is poured with a heavy hand.

★**Dorado** A large freshwater fish with white, lean firm flesh, it can exceed 20 Kg. Prized as a sports fish, called *the tiger of the river* for its spirit, but also for its fine eating. Other names are *pez amarillo, pirayú, mona,* and *monita.*

Dulces Sweets. A term often loosely applied to anything from jellies (*jalea*), preserves, sweet pastes, and candies to fruits served in syrup. The most common are *dulce de leche, de batata* and *de membrillo*.

Dulce de batata Sweet potato preserves.

✓**Dulce de leche** Caramelized milk. See "Dulce de leche" on page 18.

Dulce de membrillo
Quince preserves

Durazno Peach

E

Echalote Shallot.

✓**Empanada** A filled pastry similar to a turnover. See "Empanada" on page 18.

Endivia Endive (Belgian endive). Sometimes written *endibia*.

Enebro Juniper berry

Eneldo Dill

Ensaimada A sweet roll served for breakfast. Similar in shape and outward appearance to those popular in Mallorca, Spain, it is difficult to encounter any that are not filled with *dulce de leche*.

Ensalada Salad

Entraña Skirt steak, comparable to the French *onglet*. It is sometimes mistranslated as entrails. It is a chewy but very flavorful cut of meat. Some restaurants offer it with or without the *piel*, or skin.

Entremés Starter or appetizer.

✓**Escabeche** A marinade made with oil, vinegar and herbs.

Escarola Curly endive, escarole.

Espárrago Asparagus

Espárragos blancos White asparagus, fresh seldom available out of season (Oct.—Nov.).

Espinaca Spinach

Espinazo The beef backbone.

Estofado A type of stew where the meat is eaten apart from the sauce, such as a pot roast.

Estragón Tarragon

F

Factura The collective name for small sweet pastries. Typically Argentines will breakfast lightly with a coffee and some "*facturas*." Facturas will also be eaten in the late afternoon with coffee, mate or tea in an Argentine version of *Tea*.

Fainá A flat bread of garbanzo flour similar to a pizza, of Italian (Liguria) origin. Excellent for those who are sensitive to gluten.

Faisán Pheasant

Fariña Manioc flour or a mash made with manioc flour similar to polenta, of Guaraní origin.

Fiambres Fiambres is the common term used for "cold cuts" or cold meat preparations. Included are

Facturas, left to right, top to bottom: Palito, Manito, Medialuna de manteca, Moñito, Empanadita de hojaldre, Medialuna de grasa, Pañuelito de hojaldre, and Sacramento.

matambre rarrollado, escabeches, queso de chancho, lengua de vaca a la vinagreta, patitos de cerdo, and *arrollado de pollo.*

Fideos The term used for fresh or dry noodles or pasta, but never used for filled pastas; of Spanish-Arab (mozárabe) origin.

Filete A fillet of meat or fish.

Filete a la romano A filet of Pejerrey or Merluza, dipped in egg-flour batter, fried in hot oil and served with lemon wedges and boiled or mashed potatoes. It is a popular Argentine dish.

Filetto A tomato sauce used for pasta or meats, very different from the Italian *filetto.*

Flan Moulded custard

★**Flan Casero** Homemade custard. Almost always a very good desert. Often served with whipped cream "*con crema*" or *con dulce de leche.*

Fondos Bottoms. Normally used in connection with lettuce and artichokes.

Frambuesa Raspberry

Frito/a Fried

Fuet Thin spicy cured sausage. Originally from Catalonia.

Frutilla Strawberry

Fugazza Pizza with onion topping, corresponding to the Italian *focaccia.* Sometimes spelled *fogassa.* The version with cheese is called *fugazzeta.*

G

Galleta criollo A thin round cracker made with wheat flour, originally made in country pulperías; it spread to the cities and is

A dish of gaznates and colaciones.

a frequent accompaniment to mate.

Gallina Hen

Gallo Rooster

Ganso(a) Gander (goose)

Garbanzo Garbanzo

Garnaciones Accompanying or side dishes.

Garrapiñada Caramelized nuts. The most common are peanuts and almonds but walnuts can be found in regions such as Mendoza where they are grown. Usually sold by ambulatory vendors on street corners and plazas, especially during winter or around Christmas and New Years.

Gaznates Pastry cone, flavored with brandy and filled with dulce de leche.

Golosina A general term for sweets or candies.

Granadero Grenadier, rat tail fish.

Grasa Fat

Grasa de pella Lard. Fine fat extracted from the beef or pork fat of the kidneys or the diaphragm muscles.

Gratinado/a "Au gratin," used for dishes which have bread crumbs and grated cheese sprinkled on top and browned under a source of high heat.

Grillé Grilled. Cooked on a grill.

Grosella Currant

Guaba Guava

Guabiyú The fruit of a tree that grows in the subtropical region of Argentina, Brazil, Bolivia, Paraguay and Uruguay. Of a deep, almost black purple color, it is sweet, slightly acid and eaten fresh.

Guanaco The native Argentine cameloid which was a principal source of meat for the indigenous Argentines. Its use was supplanted by beef after the arrival of the colonists and the subsequent development of free ranging cattle. Efforts are underway to raise guanacos commercially for their fine wool and the meat. Requirements for raising such animals are very strict. See "Ñandú" on page 41. It is offered on some *estancias*.

Guanacos

Guavirá (Gabiroba) The fruit of a tree that grows in the subtropical region of Argentina and Brazil. Green-yellow skinned fruit that looks like a small guava. Pulp is sweet and

35

high in vitamins. Eaten fresh or used to make juices, ices, liqueurs and sweets.

Guinda A type of cherry which is less sweet and more acidic than *cerezas*. Used in cooking and as a base for *aguardientes*.

Guisadilla A sweet typical of the Northwest, consisting of a light biscuit, filled with *dulce de leche*, *dulce de membrillo*, or *dulce de cayote*. Also known as *quesadilla* or *quisadilla*.

Guiso A stew cooked in a pot for a long time. Generally based on meats, cereals, beans and vegetables. Typical *guisos* are *locro*, and *chupín*.

Guiso carrero One of the legendary stews prepared by the gauchos incorporating a mix of rice, noodles and *charqui*, all of which could be carried by the gaucho for long periods of time.

H

Haba Lima bean.

Hamburguesa Hamburger. If listed among the "*platos*" do not expect a hamburger sandwich. It will be a ground meat patty served with vegetables.

Harina Flour.

★**Helado** Ice cream; see "Ice Cream" on page 75.

Higo Fig.

Hinojo Fennel.

Hongos Mushrooms.

Horno, al Cooked in the oven.

Horneado/a Baked, as in "*empanadas horneadas*."

Huascha Locro A variation of "*locro*" which includes corn, beans and onion. From the Quechua, meaning "*almost*" locro.

Huesillo A sun dried peach.

Huevos Eggs.

Huevos quimbos

Huevos quimbos A rich old fashioned dessert of baked beaten egg yolks in syrup. Sometimes spelled "*huevos chimbos*."

Huevos rellenos Stuffed eggs. The most common preparations involve mixing the yolks with tuna, parsley, anchovies or some other ingredient before refilling the cavity.

Humita A preparation of freshly grated corn kernels not unlike a corn flour dumpling. Includes mashed squash in some areas. See "Humita" on page 20. Almost always served *en chala*, corn husks.

I-K

Iñame *Batata*, the true yam. An important food

Humita en Chala.

item in Corrientes, Misiones and Paraguay.

Ingredientes An array of snacks, cheese cubes, etc. served with drinks (used in Northwest.)

Jamón Ham

... cocido Cooked ham

... crudo Cured ham

... de York Ham cooked on the bone

... Prosciutto Imported ham cured in the style of Parma, Italy. Very expensive.

... Serrano Ham cured in the style of the Spanish Serrano ham.

Jamon con melón Slices of melon served with very thin slices of cured ham. The contrasts of flavors and sweet and salty make for a delightful way to start a meal.

Jarabe Syrup

Jengibre Ginger

Kinoto Kumquat. *Quinoto* is a variant.

L

Langosta Lobster; same word is used for grasshoppers.

Langostino Prawn

★**Langostino a la milanesa** Breaded and lightly sauteed prawns. An exceptional dish if prepared in Patagonia using langostinos from the area near Rawson.

Laurel, hojas de Bay leaves

Leche Milk

... descremada Reduced fat (i.e., skimmed milk).

... entero Whole milk

... ultra pasteurizada Has undergone ultra high temperature pasteurization and has a long shelf life if unopened.

Leche asada A dessert of Spanish origin, similar to a flan.

Leche quemada A dessert of Spanish origin, popular in the Northeast, it is a baked custard that once cooked, is cooled, topped with ample sugar, then marked with a hot iron to caramelize the sugar before being served.

Lechuga Lettuce

... común Iceberg lettuce

... cono roble rojo Red oak leaf lettuce

... cono roble verde Oak leaf lettuce

... criolla An Argentine variety similar to romaine.

... mantecosa Butterhead lettuce.

... morada Red leaf lettuce

... romana Romaine lettuce

Lechón Suckling pig

Lechón adobado A *lechón* covered with an *adobo*, for several hours before being cooked in a clay oven, frequently one normally used to bake bread. This Spanish colonial preparation is common throughout the Andes. See "Cuchi" on page 32.

Lenguado Fluke or flounder; a lean white fish with firm, delicate flesh. Although lenguado is often translated as sole, the species grouped under this popular name correspond to the larger flat fish commonly referred to as plaice or *flounder*.

Lengua a la vinagreta
Sliced boiled cows tongue, dressed with a vinaigrette consisting of vinegar, oil, parsley and other herbs and spices. A popular preparation.

Lenteja Lentil

Leverwurst Liverwurst. A soft, spreadable encased cooked sausage with smoked characteristic, containing pork livers plus smoked jowls and bacon ends.

Lima Lime

Limón Lemon

Lisa Mullet. A sweet tasting flaky fleshed fish whose drawback is that it is bony, and for the sports fisherman, difficult to catch.

Loco Abalone

Locro A type of stew. See "Locro" on page 21.

Lomo Loin

Lomo de cerdo Pork loin; often available as "*ahumado*," a lightly cured or smoked form.

Lomito A popular sandwich made with a thin steak grilled and served in in an appropriately sized roll of french bread with sliced tomato, lettuce and other ingredients.

M

Magret (de pato) Duck breast

Macis Mace

Maicena Cornstarch

Maíz Maize, corn

Maíz pisingallo Dried kernels of maize. Used for making popcorn or in pre-

A lechon on display ready to be carved for someone's dinner.

paring other dishes after being rehydrated.

Mandarina Tangerine

Mandioca *Manioc, cassava,* and *yucca* are some of the other names for this plant which has a long root with a rough brown exterior and a white interior. Principally grown in Misiones, and to a much lesser degree in Formosa, Corrientes and Chaco, the root is high in carbohydrates, proteins, calcium and vitamin C. It is the source of manioc flour and tapioca.

Manduvá Manduba, a fresh-water catfish esteemed for its very fine flavor; caught along the shore of the Paraná and Riachos rivers. A similar fish is the *mandubí* or *manduví.*

Mango Mango

Maní Peanut

Manteca Butter

Mantecol A semi-hard sweet made with a paste of ground peanuts and sugar. It can be uncoated or coated with chocolate. Although the name is trademarked by Cadbury, many Argentines make their own version and call it by the same name.

Manzana Apple

Maqui Small round red fruit, sweet and astringent, used in jellies and preserves; of Araucano origin.

Mara Patagonian hare. Not a true rabbit or hare, they can weigh as much as 16 Kilos.

★**Martineta** A Patagonian bird, similar to a quail with delicious flavor.

Masa The word used for dough for bread, pastry for empanadas and pies, mixture for cookies, or batter for crepes.

✔**Matambre** The cut of beef to be found between the hide and the ribs, corresponding to flank steak and skirt steak.

Slices of Matambre Relleno with Ensalada Rusa

Matambre relleno Stuffed flank steak, rolled up and sliced.

Mazamorra Cooked Hominy. Dried hominy is called *"maíz blanco pisado."* Served sweetened as a dessert or unsweetened as a side dish to accompany meat dishes instead of rice.

Mbaipí A type of corn-meal mash made with grated corn, *fariña* or corn-meal and cheese; of Guaraní origin. It can also be prepared in a sweet version.

Mbutucá A type of sweet tablet made from grated corn, milk and sugar.

39

✔**Medialuna** Appropriately named "half-moon," these crescent shaped pastries are the most popular in Argentina. Similar to a *croissant*, they are made with butter, *medialuna de manteca*, or with lard, *medialuna de grasa*. The common size is slightly smaller than a standard *croissant* and there are smaller ones. Slightly larger versions are used in toasted sandwiches, usually limited to fillings of ham and/or cheese.

Mejillónes Mussels

Mejorana Marjoram, closely related to oregano which is more widely available in fresh form.

Melón Melon

Melón persa Persian melon

Membrillo Quince

Merengue Meringue

Merluza Argentine Hake, *Merluza Hubbsi*. It should be noted that the hake found in the Southern Atlantic are different from their Northern cousins. In addition, while the British term for this fish is hake, the U.S. term is whiting. All of the *merluzas* are mild flavored and soft textured.

Merluza Austral Southern Hake

Merluza de Cola Longtail Hake

Merluza Negra Chilean Sea Bass, Patagonian Tooth fish

Mero Grouper/Argentine Sea Bass. It has very firm meaty texture and mild flavor.

Milanesa and pure de batata with lemon for the milanesa.

Miel Honey. In Buenos Aires it is frequently differentiated for the area of origen: Sierras de Córdoba, Buenos Aires, La Pampa, Entre Ríos, Mendoza and El Chaco. Although there are varietals based on the floral source: eucalyptus, orange, lavender and others, these are mostly exported and difficult to find in the internal market.

Milanesa See page 21.

Milanesa, a la The item has been dipped in bread crumbs before frying or sautéing.

Milanesa a la Napoli Frequently written incorrectly as "Milanesa napolitana," this refers to a breaded beef cutlet topped with a slice of cheese, ham, and tomato sauce and grilled until the cheese melts.

Milhojas General term for layered pastry filled with cream or meringue. Some versions are similar to a single serving Napoleon whereas others can be the size of a dinner plate.

Minutas A category seen on some restaurant menus indicating traditional fast foods such as an omelet or milanesa.

Mollejas A popular part of the traditional asado, demand exceeds supply and a significant number are imported from the United States, where demand is very low. There are two, the *molleja de corazón*—the rounded and more desirable pancreas, and *molleja de cogote*—the thinner thymus.

Mondongo Tripe; stomach of the cow.

Mora Mulberry.

Morcilla Black pudding; a thick blood sausage. Based on blood, fat and pork, with onion, and seasoned with salt, pepper and nutmeg, the *morcilla* is part of the traditional Argentine *parrillada*.

Morilla Morel, cypress tree mushroom.

Morocha An iron pot with three legs traditionally used by the gauchos over a wood fire in the countryside.

★**Morrones asados** Roasted red peppers with skins removed and cut into sections. Normally served dressed with olive oil.

Mortadela Garlicky sausage of Italian (Bologna) origin, very high fat content, made of ground pork and beef with small pieces of fat; some variants have green olives, others have pistachios.

Moscatel A variety of grape, very sweet. Used in making dessert wines.

Mosqueta A shortened form of Rosa Mosqueta (see page 50).

Mostaza Mustard

Mote Yellow corn treated with ashes, washed and boiled. From the Quechua *muti* meaning cooked corn. There are several mote dishes, such as *Mote Tucumano* and *Mote con huesillo*.

Mozzarella A white cheese made from the milk of a *búfala* or cow according to an Italian method of production.

Muslo (de pollo) Chicken thigh.

N

Nabo Turnip. Also used as a derogative term implying that someone is dull and unimaginative.

Ñaco A basic ingredient for country dwellers in Neuquén. Grains of wheat are toasted, then milled between stones to obtain a type of flour that is stored in leather bags. This is used in the preparation of several dishes. It is common to mix the ñaco with warm sweetened milk to eat for breakfast.

Ñame See "Iñame" on page 36.

Ñandú The South American ostrich, an important food source of the indigenous people and early settlers. Now it is a protected

A plate of ñoquis.

species. Efforts are underway to raise *ñandú* for their meat, but commercial production will take years because of Argentine laws designed to protect endangered species. The small quantities available on the market in smoked form come from animals raised in Uruguay.

Naranja Orange

Naranja ombligo Navel orange

Negro/a Black

Niño envuelto A dish of the pampas in which a piece of thin meat is rolled back upon itself with a filling of chopped hard boiled egg, onions, garlic, parsley and other herbs and spices.

Níspero Loquat. Loquats are sometimes known as "Japanese medlars" but are of a different family.

Nogada A paste made from nuts, bread crumbs, oil, vinegar and pepper.

Ñoquis Gnocchi. A pasta normally made of potato dough, sometimes incorporating spinach. An inexpensive dish traditionally served as a special on the 29th day of the month. Also used as a joking reference to "ghost employees" who only show up on that day to claim the salary for the work they did not do - the 29th being the traditional payday.

Nuez moscada Nutmeg, a spice widely used in Argentine cooking.

O

Olivos Olives

> ### Olives & Olive Oils
> Argentina, the largest grower of olives in Latin America, produces fine export-standard olive oils; the highest grade being *extra virgin*. Although restaurants will provide a pepper, oil and vinegar set for you to dress your salad, the oil will often not be olive oil but if you ask for "*aceite de oliva*," it will usually be forthcoming.

Olla Cooking pot

Olla podrida Traditional meat and vegetable stew. Many variants; one recipe calls for beef, lamb, pork, chicken, quail, sausage, beans, squash, onions, peppers, and potatoes.

Orégano Oregano

Ostra Oyster

P

Pacú A fresh-water fish. Feeds on fruits along riverbanks of the Paraná and Bermejo rivers, resulting in a sweet flavor; its pink flesh changes to mother of pearl white when cooked. Efforts underway to raise commercially.

Paella A rice dish originating from Valencia Spain, there are many variations. Although the Spanish make theirs with a short-grained rice, most Argentine versions are made with long-grained rice and are not as creamy as a result.

Palmeras A *factura* consisting of two spirals of puff pastry, creating the appearance of a palm leaf, glazed with sugar before baking cut side up, which caramelizes the sugar. Small ones are called *palmeritas*.

Palmito Commonly called heart of palm in English, they are tender shoots of a palm that grows in the north of Misiones, although much of that sold in cans comes from Brazil. Widely used in Argentine cuisine, they will be found in dishes such as *ensalada de palta con palmito* and *palmitos gratinados*. Seldom found in fresh form outside of the area where they grow.

Palometa There are several fish commonly referred to as "Palometa." The one most commonly encountered in restaurants and markets is the ocean-living, silver-colored "*palometa pintada.*" It is also the name given to several fresh-water fish, including one that is a member of the piranha

Pan dulce

family. Another "*palometa*" is the ocean-living "*palometa moteada,*" of an intense iridescent blue.

Palta Avocado. *Palta* is the Inca word for avocado. Widely available and inexpensive, avocados are used extensively in Argentine cuisine. It appears in the market in many variants. One, with a sweet flavor and difficult to find outside of Salta, is the purple fleshed *palta* of San Lorenzo.

Pamplona Beef, pork or chicken rolled and tied around a filling of vegetable and cheese which is then grilled and served hot as one piece. Of Uruguayan origen. this is not to be confused with *matambre relleno*. See "Matambre" on page 39.

Pan (de) General term for bread. The most popular breads sold in Argentina are *pan francés, de vienna, de campo, lacteado,* and *pan negro.* The following terms may be used alone or in combinations to further characterize the bread.

... alargado Long

43

... árabe Pita bread

... cereal entero Whole grain

... chapata Italian style bread (ciabatta); chewy with strong crust.

... ciabata Spelling variation of chapata.

... común White bread

... costra Bread crust is described in terms of *grue-sísima*-thick, *crocante*-crisp, *suave*-smooth, or *pareja*-even.

... criolla More like a shortbread than a loaf of bread, this is made of layers of pastry dough made with lard or butter.

... de 5 cereales Five cereals - used to describe bread containing the following cereals: *maíz*-corn, *cebada*-barley, *centeno*-rye, *trigo*-wheat, and *avena*-oats.

... de campo Country bread. A large round loaf with a crisp crust, like that which would be obtained by baking in a large brick oven once common in the country.

... de semillas Seeds of *amapola*-poppy, *girasol*-sunflower, *lino*-flax, *sésamo*-sesame, and *trigo*-wheat.

... flautita Long and thin, like a flute.

... francés French style bread, normally in a long narrow loaf.

... gris Whole wheat

... integral Whole wheat

... miga esponjosa Light sandwich bread.

... miga Bread crumbs, also used to refer to the cooked dough in a loaf of bread. Thus: *sandwich de miga* means a sandwich made with crustless bread.

... molde Baked in a rectangular pan or loaf, always precut - sandwich bread.

... pebete Bread baked in an elongated shape for sandwiches for hot dogs or sausages.

... rallado Bread crumbs

... redondo Round loaf

... zepelín Oval shaped like a zeppelin.

Pan de carne Meat loaf. A popular preparation of the pampas, made using the less desirable parts of beef ground or cut into small pieces, and mixed with eggs, bread crumbs, and flavorings before being baked in a loaf pan.

Pan dulce A sweet bread containing candied fruits and nuts, similar to a Panettone. Although availability increases with the approach of Christmas, it can be found during other times of the year. Small ones of individual serving size are sold in some *panaderías*.

Pan de indio A tree-growing mushroom found in Patagonia and Tierra del Fuego.

Pancho The term is used both for the Argentine version of the hot dog and a sandwich using it. The Argentine version more closely resembles a Vienna sausage than the American hot dog, although they are

Pan de indio growing on a tree in Tierra del Fuego.

both normally served the same way, in a bun, with ketchup and mustard, or *salsa golf*.

Pancitos Rolls

Panettone A sweet bread containing candied fruit; of Italian origin.

Panzas Gizzards

Panqueque Very thin pancake, crepe. English speakers often confuse it with the "*tortita*" discussed page 52.

Papa Potato. Listed below are the most common Argentine varieties, although most stores do not mark the variety of potato.

... andina Andean potatoes. Always available in certain communities, such as those where Bolivian immigrants live, varieties of indigenous potatoes started appearing in other markets in Buenos Aires in the late 90s, marking a resurgence in interest in indigenous foods.

... Ballenera White flesh. The full name is *Bonaerense la Ballenera MAA*.

... blanca Washed potatoes from Cordoba or Mendoza; generally from variety Spunta.

... Frital INTA White flesh, excellent fried, very good boiled or mashed.

... Huinkul Mag Common variety, recommended for boiling and mashed potatoes.

... Kennebec Has a pale thin skin, white flesh, very good fried, also good boiled or mashed.

... negra Non-washed potatoes from the Southeast region of Buenos Aires Province with the typical black soils adhered to the skin.

... Pampeana INTA White flesh, very good boiled or mashed.

... procesada :Washed potatoes from the Southeast region of Buenos Aires Province that imitate the skin finish of the Cordoba or Mendoza potatoes with some powder (soil mix) added after drying.

... Spunta Yellow fleshed potato

Pargo Blanco Argentine Croaker. Lean white meat that's tender and full-flavored.

Pargo Rosado Red Snapper. Low in fat; flaky white flesh.

Pasas Dried fruit. Used by itself means raisins. Others are *pasas de durazno* and *pasas de damasco* which are quite popular among the Arab immigrants living in La Rioja, Catamarca, and Tucumán.

Pascualina An Easter speciality of Northern Italy which has been widely adopted in Argentina. Also called *torta pascualina* or *torta de Pascua*. Consists of

Andean potatoes in a Bolivian market in Buenos Aires.

many layers of fine pastry layered with a mixture of chard, spinach, arugula, goat cheese and herbs.

Pasta A general term for pasta dishes, it also means paste, e.g., *pasta de tomate*, tomato paste or *pasta de dientes*, tooth paste. As a matter of curious interest, a reputable Argentine travel guidebook recommends using *pasta de dulce de membrillo* for emergency repairs of gasoline tank leaks, which occur frequently when traveling ripian roads.

Pastafrola A pie believed to be based upon the Austrian Linzer Torte; with a sweet butter-egg crust filled with something sweet such as *dulce de frambuesa* and topped with a lattice or *enrejado* of the same dough before being baked.

Pastel A pastry shell which is filled with a savory or sweet filling. The shell and filling can be baked together or the shell can be baked before being filled.

… de boda Wedding cake

… de chocolate Chocolate cake.

… de papas Shepherds pie. See "Pastel de Papas" on page 109.

… de pollo Chicken pie

Pastelito Filled pastries; normally filled with *dulce de membrillo, de batata,* or *de leche,* although others can be used.

Patas Legs.

Patasca A stew prepared with tripe and pig or lamb trotters. One version uses calves feet from which the meat is scraped before serving.

Patay A traditional sweet of Córdoba and Santiago del Estero. Prepared using the beans of the algarrobo tree, which are ground to create a paste that is formed into thin round disks and dried in brick ovens.

Patitas de cerdo (cordero) Pigs (lambs) feet

Patitas aliñadas Marinated leg of beef, veal, pork or lamb, depending on context.

Pato Duck

Patí A fresh-water fish found in the River Plate basin. Up to 3 Kg. Also known as *bagre plateado* and *patí rojizo*.

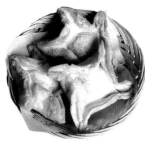
Pastelitos

Pava A wild bird resembling the female of the domesticated turkey whose habitat is the forests and humid woods of Northern Argentina.

Pavita Domesticated turkey. Unlike many animals, the same name is used in Argentina for the male and female, although the meat of the male is drier and more fibrous.

Pebete See *Pan Pebete*.

Pecarí A wild mammal with an aspect similar to the European *jabalí* (boar) and pigs.

Pechuga Breast

Pejerrey A relatively slender fish with white flaky flesh and a delicate flavor. Abundant in Argentine waters, there are two freshwater subspecies and a marine one.

Pelón Nectarine

Peludo A type of armadillo, it is considered very good eating by those who live in the countryside and is frequently offered for sale preserved in escabeche in artesanal markets. Also called *piche* in some areas.

Pepinillo Cornichon (small variety of cucumber used for pickles in France).

Pepino Cucumber

Pepino inglés Long thin variety of cucumber.

Pera Pear

Perca Perch. This sports fish is abundant in Argentine waters and its flavorful flaky white flesh is prized by fishermen. Sometimes referred to as the *trucha criolla*.

Perdiz Partridge

Perejil Parsley. Most parsley is of the flat leaf variety frequently referred to as Italian parsley.

Pescadilla In Argentine waters, there are two *pescadillas*, the *pescadilla de red* and *pescadilla real*. Both belong to the family Sciaenidae, whose members are known as drums or croakers. The flesh is lean and flaky when cooked.

Pez Angel Angelfish shark

Pez Espada Swordfish. Usually comes as firm, boneless steaks with a firm meaty texture and rich but mild taste. Color varies from ivory white to slightly pink.

Pez Gallo Elephant Fish

Pez Limón Yellow tail, Amberjack.

Picada Selection of tapas or little nibbles, served with beer or wine. Some can be quite large. A *picada de mariscos*, for example can serve as a meal for two to four people.

Picante Hot

Pimentón Paprika

Pimienta Pepper

Pimienta de cayena Cayenne pepper.

Pimiento Pepper, usually used to refer to sweet bell pepper; common varieties sold locally are:

... **Calahora** Medium, red pepper with pointed end; roasted and packed in jars this is the well known pimiento.

... **Colorado** Large, often sold in yellow variant.

... **Morrón** Large, sweet thick flesh, very good for salads and roasting, sold in green (immature) and red (mature).

... **rojo dulce** Red sweet pepper.

Piña Pineapple. Preferred term in Argentina is *ananá*.

Pino, hongo Bolete, cepe, porcini mushroom.

Piñónes Pine nuts. A flavorful addition to salads and other dishes.

Pionono A sweet or savory filled rolled cake. Used to refer to the sheet of cake which can be purchased ready to use.

✔**Pionono de camarones** Savory rolled cake with prawn and *palmito* filling, served in slices.

Pionono de camarones

Pirco A stew of beans, corn, pork bones and bacon.

Pitanga The fruit of a tree in the Northeastern forests with many local names: Ñangapirí, Surinam Cherry, Brazilian Cherry, Cayenne Cherry. Small, 1" around, shiny red to black fruit with prominent lobes. Flesh is juicy, with an acid to sweet flavor. Can be eaten fresh or as a preserve.

Pochoclo Popcorn. Argentines prefer sweetened form over salted and buttered version.

Polaca Southern Blue Whiting.

Polenta A dish based on corn flour (meal) cooked in water or milk. Of Italian origin, it is of such wide use in Argentina that instant polenta, based on precooked corn flour, can be purchased in stores throughout. Served soft, or after drying, cut into rectangles and fried or grilled. In both cases, topped with a sauce, most commonly tomato or mushroom.

Pollitos bebes Pullets (young chickens).

Pollo Chicken

... **eviserado** Gutted

... **sin menudos** Without giblets

Polvo de hornear Baking powder

Polvorones A traditional cracker made from wheat flour, sugar and fat, cooked in the oven until dry and crispy. Generally served with tea or mate.

Pomelo Grapefruit

Poroto General term for bean

... blancos Lima bean

... colorado Red bean

... negro Black bean

... seca Dried bean

... soja Soy bean

Postres Desserts

Provenzal, a la A dish prepared with olive oil, garlic and parsley "in the style of Provence."

Puchero The Argentine version of the French *"pot au feu"* or the Spanish *"cocido."* A traditional boiled meat and vegetable dish, cooked slowly in one pot which is served in two or three courses: the broth as a soup, followed by the vegetables and the meats. This is a filling dish, best on cold days. See recipe on page 109.

Puerro Leek

Pulpo Octopus

Puré Mashed or pureed. *Puré de zapallo* is deservedly served as frequently as *puré de papas.*

Q

Queso Cheese. See "Cheeses" on page 17.

Quesú Cambá A typical Paraguayan dish that has expanded into the Northeast of Argentina, especially in Misiones and northern Corrientes. A type of stew that uses local ingredients, always fresh corn kernels and fresh cheese. Prepared in clay pots, it is finished in the oven to brown the top.

Quibebe A creamy zapallo preparation popular in the northeast and Brazil; with many variations, some spicy, some with meat or cheese.

Quinua Quinoa; Andean cereal, very high in protein.

Quinoto Kumquat. *Kinoto* is a variant.

R

Raba Large squid cut into rings for frying.

Rábano picante Horseradish

Rábano Radish

Radicchio Red chicory

Radicheta A type of chicory, a small leaf, slightly bitter salad green.

Ramita Stalk

Raya Ray, skate. Rays prefer to eat mollusks, crustaceans and small fish, which give their flesh a sweet mild shellfish-like taste.

Rebanada (de pan) Slice (of bread)

Relleno Stuffed

Remolacha Beet

Repollo Cabbage

Repostería Section in supermarkets dealing with baking, pastry, and confectionary.

Repollo Bruselas Brussels sprouts

Revuelto Scrambled eggs. See "Revuelto Gramajo" on page 21.

Risotto A creamy textured rice dish of Northern Italian origen; there are innumerable variations.

Róbalo Sea Bass, Patagonian icefish

Rocio de miel Honeydew

Rojo/a Red

Romana, al la The item has been lightly dipped in flour before being fried or sauteed.

Romero Rosemary

Ropa vieja Thinly sliced beef cooked in a tomato sauce.

Rosa mosqueta Rose hip, used in Patagonian preserves and jellies.

Rosada Reddish or rose

Rosca de Reyes Large ring sweet bread traditionally served for *Reyes*, Epiphany. Of Spanish origin, there are many variants, some topped with a sugar glaze, chopped nuts and fruits.

Roscas Bread roll baked in the shape of a ring

... rellenas Filled. *Roscas rellenas* are customarily filled with marzipan.

Roscón Large ring-shaped bun, often containing fruit and nuts.

Rubio Red gunard. A tasty marine fish caught along the Argentine continental shelf.

Rúcula Arugula, a bitter salad green.

S

Salmón de Mar Brazilian Sand perch. Also sold as *salmón blanco*.

Salmón rosado Salmon. Farm raised salmon with a pink flesh similar to that found in European and U.S. markets.

Salmonete Red Mullet

Salmuera Brine

Salpicón A vegetable salad to which some red or white meat has been added, dressed with a very simple mayonnaise, and served cold or at room temperature. See recipe on page 107.

Salsa Sauce. Some sauces frequently encountered in stores or on menus are:

... Bolognesa In the style of Bologna Italy, a tomato sauce containing meat.

... Golf A mayonnaise and ketchup sauce that is very popular in Argentina.

... Portuguesa A tomato sauce that includes red peppers.

... Napolitana A tomato sauce that contains green and black olives.

... Puttanesca Similar to the Napolitana.

... Scrofa A pinkish sauce based on a filetto sauce mixed with cream, basil and cheese.

Verde A green spinach cream sauce.

Salvia Sage

Sandía Water melon

Sándwich de miga Crustless sandwiches made of thinly sliced white bread with combinations of thinly sliced ham, cheese, tomato or with thin spreads of tuna or chicken salad. Always two full sandwiches. Often a choice of *simple* or *triple* will be available. *Simple* is a plain sandwich; *triple* consists of three slices of bread with two layers of filling.

Sargo Bream

Savorin A coastal fish, with a strong flavor, high in omega 3 oils. Mostly exported, so seldom seen on Argentine menus.

Sauco Elderberry.

Seviche Fresh fish or shellfish cooked by the action of the acid in lime or lemon juice, flavored with various fresh herbs. Believed to originate with the Incas of Ecuador or Peru, every Latin American country seems to have its own version. Also spelled *ceviche* and *cebiche.*

Shitake Shiitake mushroom

Sobrasada A soft, fatty fresh red pork sausage, seasoned with paprika. Introduced by Spanish immigrants from Mallorca.

Sopa Soup

Sopa Paraguaya. Not a soup at all, this is a creamy corn flour casserole dish. *Sopa norteña* is a similar dish.

Sopresata An Italian-style cured sausage similar to pepperoni.

Sorbete con champaña A popular dessert offering consisting of sherbet, most frequently lemon, served in a tall glass bathed in champagne.

Spiedo, al On the spit. Normally used for meat which is cooked on a rotating spit.

Stolen German or Nordic style sweet bread, always contains bits of dried or candied fruit, sometimes contains marzipan.

Supreme (de pollo) Chicken breast

✔**Surubí** A large fresh-water fish found in the Paraná-Uruguay river basin. A member of the bagre family. Prized for its flavor.

T

Tabla de quesos A plate of mixed cheeses.

Tamal Similar to a humita, except that it is filled with a spiced meat and vegetable mixture. See "Humita" on page 20. Almost always served *en chala* (in corn husks).

Tapa In Argentina, *tapa* is used to refer to the ready-to-use rounds of pastry sold in stores as a labor-saving convenience for making pies, empanadas and cocktail-sized empanadas. Only in Spanish restaurants and bars is it used in the Spanish sense as a collective term for little things to eat with your drink.

Tarta The terms *pastel* and *tarta* are confusing and too frequently loosely used, to the point one is never certain what is exactly offered on the menu. Strictly speaking, a *tarta* is a large *pastel* or cake with a sweet or savory filling. See "Pastel" on page 46.

Tiburón Shark

Tira de asado Strip of ribs, usually served as a small portion cut from that strip.

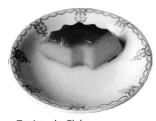

Tocino de Cielo.

Tocino de Cielo A rich, very sweet dessert made from egg yolks and sugar, with a consistency similar to flan. The name meaning heavenly bacon comes from its resemblance to a slab of bacon due to the caramelized sugar on top. A traditional dessert of the Northwest, of Spanish origin.

Tomate Tomato

Tomaticán A tomato and vegetable stew.

Tomillo Thyme

Torta A cake, usually round.

Torta frita Fried dough, similar to the Mexican sopaipilla.

Torta galesa A dark spicy cake with candied fruit created by the Welsh settlers in Patagonia. There is no similar cake in Wales. Also known as *Torta negra galesa*.

Tortita Breakfast pancake. See "Panqueque" on page 45.

Tostado/a Literally, toast. When term is used in combination with *"queso, jamon*, etc., refers to toasted sandwich, normally of thin slices of *pan de miga*. This is such a popular request that common usage is to call for a *tostado* or *tostado mixto* to order a toasted ham and cheese sandwich.

Tostones Thick slices of bread topped with a combination of ingredients. Similar to a *bruscheta*.

Traviata A flat, mild flavored crisp biscuit, often used as a canape base for spreading soft cheeses or pates.

Triolet Trio of little snack crackers served with drinks.

Trucha Trout

Tuco Tomato sauce for pastas or meats

Turrón A soft candy very similar to the Italian nougat.

U

Ubajay The yellow globular fruit of a tree in the humid subtropical forests of Argentina, Brazil, Uruguay and Paraguay. Edible but has a disagreeable odor; eaten fresh or preserved.

Untar, untable Spread, spreadable (of jam or other potted mixes.)

Uva Grape

V

Vacuno/a Bovine (adjective), pertaining to cattle.

Vaina de vainilla Vanilla bean

Vainilla Vanilla

Verdeo, al Cooked or served with a sauce containing green onions.

Verduras Vegetables

Vianda Sandwich/box lunch

Vieira Scallops. Sold in the shell, *entera*, on the half shell, *media valva,* or as scallops, *cayos.*

Vigilante A dessert of fresh white cheese with a fruit preserve, normally quince *membrillo* but others such as *batata, cayote* and *honey* are also used.

✓**Vizcacha** A small animal similar to a prairie dog, but no relation. Considered to be very succulent.

Violeta Violet

Y

Yemas (de huevo) Egg yolk

Yemas quemadas A rich dessert of the Northwest based on egg yolks and sugar.

Yogur Yogurt

Bags of "zapallos"

Yogur natural Natural yogurt

Yopará A dish containing *charque*, hominy, beans, manioc, *batatas* and onion.

Yuca Yucca

Z

Zanahoria Carrot

Zapallo General term used for squash. Encompasses pumpkins and hard winter squashes.

... anco Butternut squash, most common variety sold

... coreano Similar to anco

... largo Long, more closely resembles vegetable marrow, zucchini or courgettes.

... redondo Globe squash, or round vegetable marrow or zucchini. Also called *Zapallito.*

Zarzamora Blackberry

Zarzaparrilla Sarsaparilla

Wine & Drink of Argentina

Introduction

Argentina is a major world wine producer, fifth in the world in consumption and production. Its vineyards stretch all along the base of the Andes range from Salta in the North to Patagonia in the South, over 1600 kilometers in length but narrow in width. Argentina is the only serious wine producer in the world with a Continental climate and heights that range between 400 to 3000 meters above sea level.

These features, added to the fact that over 90% of the vineyards depend on irrigation for survival, give Argentine wine production a very special characteristic that has only recently been fully understood and developed. Argentine wines are now being exported worldwide with many winning important medals and effusive reviews.

In addition to wine, Argentines drink a lot of beer made locally. Imported beers are scarce at the time of writing due to the economic situation. Other alcoholic drinks of local production include whiskey, vodka, rum and vermouth. Sherry and port type wines are produced but are little drunk.

Soft drinks are big business as are different types and grades of milk and yogurt beverages. The drinking of coffee and tea is popular, and of course there is the indigenous beverage, Yerba Mate.

Above—The cellars of Bodega Finca Flichman
Left—Café Dorrego, Plaza Dorrego, San Telmo, Buenos Aires
Preceding—Café Britanico, San Telmo, Buenos Aires
p54—Harvesting grapes in Mendoza

Wine

History of Argentine
Wine When the Spanish explorers arrived here, there were neither vineyards nor wild grape vines. It was in 1554 that Padre Cedrón planted the first cuttings in Santiago del Estero, supposedly to provide the church with the wine necessary for Mass, and wine has been in continuous production ever since. By 1594 wine was being exported from La Rioja to Potosí, Bolivia.

However, wine production remained a cottage industry until expertise and technical support was provided under the administration of President Sarmiento, who founded three agricultural schools to improve the agriculture of the Cuyo. At the head of each school, he installed an expert: a Frenchman, an Italian and a German. These schools provided a

base for further and gradual improvements, but it was around the turn of the 19th Century with the increase in immigration, and wealth of the country that saw Argentine wine making really take off.

As immigrants arrived at the docks in Buenos Aires, those with winemaking experience soon found themselves enroute to the vineyards on the foothills of the Andes, primarily to Mendoza, but also to Salta, Rio Negro and other wine growing regions. These immigrants brought with them not only their skills, but also their preferences for certain grape varieties and styles which also helped meet the preferences of the other immigrants for the wines with which they were familiar. As a result, Argentina produces a wider range of wines than European countries.

Thus there was a period of rapid growth until some time after the great period of immigration. The economic and social conditions reigning in the country, particularly those of the 1960s and 1970s, resulted in a preference for grape and wine quantity over quality. Argentina's wine production was

A bottle of Etchart's premium wine in a special presentation box.

Looking across the roof of Michel Torino Bodega La Rosa.

directed toward meeting internal demand, not competing in the fine wine export market.

However, in the 1980s, a transformation of the whole wine-making industry began. Not only the planting of better varieties but also the implementation of improved, modern wine production methods, enabled Argentina to take its rightful place in the world of fine wine producing countries. This transformation process not only required time and leadership but also money. Recognizing the potential, respected vintners from France, Italy, and the United States started making investments. Some, bought into existing Argentine wineries. Some

bought land and started their own operations under an Argentine label. A few have planted vines with the stated intention of shipping the product elsewhere for processing.

Whatever the intention and process, the result has been a transformation of the wine industry. Argentina's wines are competitive across the board, from fine world-class wines to inexpensive ones.

Wine Regions The provinces of Mendoza and San Juan produce between them over 90% of the total wine of Argentina (averaging 18-19 million hectoliters[1] per year) thanks to

1. 1 hectoliter equals 100 liters.

their ideal soil and climate. Twelve other provinces also produce significant quantities of wine, with La Rioja, Rio Negro and Salta being the most important. For further information, see *"Wineries to visit. Wines to taste"* on page 115.

Varieties Grown While almost 50 different grape varietals are cultivated to a greater or lesser degree, Argentina possesses two varietals that can almost be called its own. The first is a white grape, the Torrontés, whose origins are questioned although most authorities accept the northwest corner of Spain (Galicia) as the most likely spot. The other grape is a red of French origin, the Malbec (also known as Cot in Cahors) which, like the Torrontés, has found in Argentina ideal conditions for developing into grapes that make truly superior wines. Other major varietals are the Cabernet Sauvignon, Chardonnay, Syrah, Merlot, Semillón and Chenin, with a mob of lesser cultivated grape varieties such as Pinot Noir, Viognier, Bonarda and others pressing forward to obtain a spot in the cellar.

In 1970 wine consumption in Argentina stood at

91 liters per capita per annum. Much of it was table or common wine (*vino común*) and drunk with soda water added. Around the 1980s, an endeavor was undertaken to improve wine quality and increase exports. At the same time, consumption started to fall (almost all of it *vino común*) and fine wines began to appear, many aimed at the export market. Per capita consumption is now at around 38 liters.

Today Argentina is a minor but increasingly significant exporter. Its top market is the United kingdom, followed by Europe and the US. The wine which has led the field has been the Malbec, considered to be the best in the world. Other important exports are the Merlot and Cabernet-Sauvignon, with Syrah becoming an important newcomer. Numerous important prizes and medals are regularly obtained by any Argentine wines at the many wine events held worldwide.

Wineries (Bodegas) There are over 1100 regulated wineries or *"bodegas"* in Argentina, and some 25 of these produce about 90% of the finest and most successful labels. A short list of the most important includes the following: Canale, Chandon, Etchart, Fabre Montmayor, Flichman, La Rural, Lopez, Luigi Bosca, Nieto Sentiner, Norton, Ricardo Santos, Salentein, San Felicien, Catena, Santa Julia, Familia Zucardi, and Trapiche. The system used to distinguish between a bodega's premium and ordinary wines is not standardized and since the economic crisis of 2002 with a greater focus on the export market, is in a state of flux.

DOC A strict system of labeling and quality control in the production of wines, similar to the *Appellation Controlée* as used in France or *Denominacion de Origen Controlada* (DOC) in Spain is only now beginning to evolve in Argentina, which is the only Latin American country to have one. Parts of Mendoza, including the southern region of San Rafael and the Upper Rio Negro Valley have introduced DOC regulations that are slowly being adopted by more and more wineries. The letters DOC on a label indicate wines that have been made in accordance with local quality wine regulations.

Vintages Vintage charts and the talk of which year was a good, poor or excellent one can be considered a good guide but little more since there are so many factors which influence the quality of wine. Especially, the quality depends on the skill of a winemaker to use his prime material, the grape, correctly. There are many who believe the vintage does not matter since so much of Argentina's grape production relies on irrigation. Nevertheless there are variations in quality from year to year.

The Argentine Instituto Nacional de Tecnología Agropecuaria, (INTA), studied the climatic variables that influence grape quality, and used these to develop a model, collect data and predict the average quality of the vintage. These factors are similar to

Mendoza Vintages

The below is only an indicator as to the average quality of wine produced that year.

Year	Red	White
1996	Excellent	Excellent
1997	Good	Good
1998	Poor-Good	Poor
1999	Excellent	Excellent
2000	Poor	Poor
2001	Good	Excellent
2002	Good	Poor
2003	Excellent	Very Good
2004	Ex -VG	Excellent

those in other wine producing regions, save soil humidity, and include such things as maximum and minimum temperatures during different periods of growth, number and length of sunny days, to name a few. INTA then used them to develop a vintage chart for Argentine wines.

Beer

Argentines are great beer drinkers, consumption being second only to wine in the alcoholic beverage category. The style is almost exclusively lager, ales and speciality beers being hard to find. However, a small but growing presence of micro breweries is making itself felt and could become important soon.

Quilmes is the leading beer manufacturer in Argentina, followed by Isenbeck (of German Warsteiner origin) and Brahma (of Brazilian origin). Recently Quilmes sold a major stake to Brahma.

According to Bob Klein ("Beer Lover's Rating Guide") the best beer in Argentina is Bierkert Especial (Bieckert brewery), a Pilsner style beer, with a rating of 4.2 on a scale of 5. In second place he puts Santa Fe Rubia Especial (Santa Fe brewery), a lager style beer with a 3.9 rating.

Yerba Mate

One of the most traditional and typical drinks of Argentina (shared with Paraguay, Uruguay and Southern Brazil) is mate. Known abroad as the South American green tea, "yerba" signifies herb in Spanish and "mate" is gourd in the Quechua lan-

A "mate" bush with leaves ready to harvest.

which are stored for a period ranging from three to nine months with the longer time reserved for the higher quality leaves which results in a more expensive form of yerba mate. At the end of the process, the leaves and sticks are crushed and filtered to a small size before being bagged for sale and consumption.

Mate can be prepared and drunk exactly like tea, including the modern use of sachets, or in the traditional manner with the dried leaves and stalks in the mate gourd and drunk through a tube, known as a *"bombilla."*

guage. However, the Guaraní natives of Paraguay, now believed to have been the first consumers of the herb called it *"kaa-guazú"* which means "splendid plant." They were wont to chew the leaves raw (as coca leaves are chewed today) but the arrival of the Jesuits imposed its use as an infusion. This provided the Jesuits with a lucrative trade, particularly as the colonists began to adopt to drinking mate.

Yerba mate is grown on plantations where the leaves are harvested along with the small branches or stalks holding the leaves. The leaves and the stalks are subjected to a brief period of high heat to stop the oxidation, followed by a longer period of lower heat to dry the leaves. They are then stuffed into huge breathable bags

A woman sipping mate through a bombilla on a Sunday afternoon in the park.

"Mate is in use in every house all day long and the compliment of the country is to hand the mate cup and tube serving for all, and an attendant being kept in wait-

ing to replenish for every person." So wrote English traveller Emeric Essex Vidal in 1820. This ceremony remains pretty much unchanged today, particularly in the countryside.

Mate should be made with water that is almost, but not, boiling (80° C or 150°F is optimum) and no sugar. Less demanding and classic consumers veer from the authentic by adding sugar and or other flavors such as orange peel, herbs and even a pinch of coffee.

Wine and Food Routes

The concept of wine routes, to which food routes are being annexed, is relatively new to Argentina. Argentina still does not have anything comparable to Germany, France, California, South Africa or Australia, but there are some interesting opportunities and growing interest.

The province of Mendoza offers several different routes adopted to the time available and the interest of the visitor. 80 of the 1200 bodegas in Mendoza accept visitors in varying degrees. Offered are guided visits, lunches, tastings, wine courses and, a recent addition, lodging at the *bodega*. One caution to the visitor, the siesta is sacred in Mendoza, and you need to plan other activities for the period 2 PM to 4 PM. For more information get a copy of "Wineries to visit. Wines to taste," (see page 115.)

In addition to wine routes, Mendoza has (to date) four food routes. The routes offer more than the name suggests with lodging, dining, horseback riding, and other activities available.

• **Camino Criollos**—Creole Route; typical Mendozan products such as asado, locro, empanadas, etc.

• **Huella de los Caprinos**—Literally in the footsteps of the goat, this route deals with locations specializing in goat products, such as goat cheese or roast goat.

• **Olivares del sol**—Olive Groves of the Sun; Olives and olive oil.

• **Ruta de Frutas y Aromas**—Route of Fruits and Aromas; Fresh fruit, preserves, honey and herbs.

Looking beyond the observatory El Leoncito towards the Andes at sunrise.

All of these offer an opportunity to enjoy Mendocino wine. You can find additional information through your hotel or the Mendoza Office of Tourism, or "La Fundación Instituto de Desarrollo Rural (IDR)" on page 115.

Cordoba is also developing gastronomic routes as part of a program of rural tourism. The following options are offered or under development:

• **Ruta de los chacinados y los quesos**—The route of sausages and cheeses.

• **Ruta del Cabrito y la florihorticultura**—The route of the goat and flower growing.

• **Ruta del Olivo**—Route of the olive growing.

• **Ruta de las Dulzuras de los valles Cordobeses**—The route of sweets of the Cordovan valleys.

• **Ruta de los sabores de Traslasierra**—Route of the flavors of the Sierras.

Mate and Tea routes are being organized in Corrientes and Misiones. In Tucumán, Catamarca and Salta, planning for a route covering regional wines, cheese, goats and fruit is well advanced. There is also a wine route in Rio Negro.

The nature of these routes and what tourists can do and experience will vary greatly. In Rio Negro, for example, there is no marked route and one need arrange for a guided tour. In Mendoza, the different routes offer places to stay and to eat, as well as bodegas to visit, but visiting hours at bodegas are more limited than one accustomed to wineries in France or California might expect. For the immediate future, advance planning is needed.

65

At The Bar

Cocktails

Although Argentines do not currently drink many cocktails, this is a fairly recent development for the middle and upper class. Not very long ago, Argentina was famous for its barmen and their cocktails. Ever since Enzo Antonetti, for many years barman of the Claridge Hotel, won the first world championship for Argentina, Argentina played a major role in the world of barmen. After Antonetti in 1964, Argentina won three more world championships, two vice-championships, and two or three team vice-championships. Today, and for about fifteen years, Argentina has faded from the world stage. But you would be pleasantly surprised if you

Above—The bar of the Claridge Hotel, Buenos Aires.

looked at what was offered at the bars of the better hotels and night spots.

Coffee

One legacy of the Italian immigrants is the coffee served in Buenos Aires and many other cities. Most restaurants, cafes and bars use espresso coffee machines, although unfortunately hotels generally brew large pots of strong coffee to serve their guests for breakfast. To get what you want, you need to know the standard terminology (next page).

Drink Terms

If you care for a drink before a meal, at a bar, or arrange for drinks at home, here are a few useful terms and tips.

Abrelatas Can opener.
Agua Water
... mineral Mineral water.

... con gas ... with gas, i.e., fizzy

... sin gas ... without gas

Aloja A fermented drink, mostly made from pineapple, quince, the *algarrobo* tree, etc.

Aguardiente Clear brandy or *"eau de vie,"* distilled from fermented fruit juice. The *aguardiente* of Catamarca is distilled from wine.

Aperitivo Apéritif, a drink typically consumed before a meal; commonly produced with bitter herbs, stalks and roots. Some are based on wine, such as Vermouth.

Balde para hielo Ice bucket.

Balon A large balloon shaped glass, usually used for beer.

Barril, de In the barrel, on draft, as in *cidra de barril*.

Batido A milkshake, using either ice cream or a liquid

such as chocolate as flavoring.

Boldo A characteristic Argentine drink, this herbal tea is made from the leaves of the *"Pneumus Boldo"* tree, originally from the Pantigonean Andes.

Botella Bottle.

Caipirinha A Brazilian drink popular in tropical areas of Argentina. Traditionally made with *"cachaça"*—a Brazilian cane sugar *aguardiente*, limes and sugar, there are versions using rum, vodka or tequila.

Chinato An apéritif of Argentine origin, it is based on quinine and sweet wines.

Cimarrón Bitter mate; also slang for wild dog or cattle.

Clericó A drink or cocktail of white wine with sugar and pieces of fresh fruit, such as apple, banana, pineapple, orange, peaches, etc. Sometimes prepared and served in pitchers.

Lágrima Warm milk with a *"lágrima,"* tear of coffee

Cerveza Beer.

Cerveza tirada Draft beer.

Chopp A mug or glass, smaller than a balon; usually used for serving beer, also used for cider.

Cóctel Any drinking occasion. Traditional cocktails may or may not be present.

Coctelera Cocktail shaker.

Copa Glass with stem. i.e., *copa de vino.*

> ### Coffee Terminology
>
> **Café, café espresso, café solo** All of these terms are understood to mean a small cup of espresso coffee.
>
> **Café Americano** An espresso cut with water to reduce the strength of the coffee.
>
> **... cortado** An espresso cut with a bit of steamed milk.
>
> **... con leche** Espresso with a lot of steamed milk.
>
> **... doble** A double or large coffee.
>
> **... chico** Small.
>
> **...jarrita** large espresso served in a little jug
>
> **... lágrima** Milk with a tear of coffee

Herbal Teas

The following herbal teas are commonly encountered in restaurants and stores. The formulation is as "Té de menta."

Boldo A uniquely Argentine herbal tea. Aids the function of the liver and stomach

Cedrón Based on a Peruvian plant, refreshing and calming, aids the function of the stomach.

Manzanilla Camomile. Calming, aids stomach functions

Menta Peperina Based on an Argentine mint, helps open bronchial passages, refreshes and aids stomach.

Poleo A refreshing flavor in a drink that is considered to be a digestive aid.

Tilo An herbal tea with a calming and relaxing effect.

Corcho Cork.

Exprimido Squeezed. Used to indicate juices freshly squeezed on the premises.

Gaseosa Fizzy soft drink.

Ginebra Dutch gin. "Gin" is used for English gin."

Grapa An Italian style *aguardiente*.

Guarapo A type of honey-water made by mixing honey and water and allowing it to ferment. Used by farm laborers to slake their thirst. Since they perform a lot of work in the sun, they will keep this nearby in a gourd, small keg or pot.

Hielo Ice (cubes).

Hielo granizado Crushed ice.

Infusión Herbal tea. *Infusión* is a term infrequently used in Argentina. See Té.

Jarra Jug.

Jugo Juice.

Lata Can.

Lavativa Weak, cold mate.

Leche de gallina A drink of the Northeast prepared with sweet red wine, generally *vino patero*, boiled with sugar and stick cinnamon until it starts to thicken. Although it can be drank at ambient temperature, in the higher elevations during the cold winter nights the locals generally drink it hot.

Lemoncello An alcoholic, sweet liquor made by steeping lemons and sugar in a white alcohol. Originally from Italy, it is frequently offered in Italian restaurants after the meal. The further one goes from Buenos Aires, the less likely this drink will be encountered.

Licor A sweet alcoholic drink, usually taken with dessert or pastries. Most are produced on a small scale. Those commonly prepared in the Northwest are of milk and of egg; in Patagonia, red fruit such as strawberry, cherry, and cassis are preferred; in the Northeast, orange and palm fruit. Recently *lemoncello* has become popular in the Province of Buenos Aires. Chocolate and coffee based *licors* are also popular.

Licor bottles in a shop in Gaiman.

Licuado A drink of pureed fruits. Can be prepared with juice, milk or water.

✔**Mate** Mate is the term used for both the beverage and the containers from which they are drunk; traditionally made from a gourd, they are also made from other materials and can be decorated very elaborately.

Martini An aperitif of Martini. For a gin or vodka martini one needs to ask for such.

Monacal The brand of a series of products made by the monks of the Benedictine Abbey of Niño Dios, Victoria, Entre Rios. Its liquors are neither as widely known or available as that of their French brothers in Fechamp but they are very good.

Paleta colador Strainer.

Pava tropera A broad flat bottomed tea kettle traditionally used by gauchos to heat water for mate. The broad flat bottom makes it easy to heat the water quickly.

Pisco Pisco is an Andean white brandy made from juice of the moscatel grape.

✔**Pisco Sour** An aperitif made from pisco, fresh lemon juice and sugar. it is a popular drink up and down the Andes but will seldom be encountered in the pampas.

Porrón Large bottle of beer.

Puisco A fermented drink based on corn and lemon.

Sacacorcho Corkscrew.

Soda Club soda.

Mates with bombillas and a bag of yerba mate.

Sidra Cider

✔**Submarino** A large glass of hot milk into which a bar of bitter chocolate is submerged and left to slowly dissolve.

Té Tea; Argentina grows real tea in Misiones and Corrientes. This plus a wide range of herbal teas or infusions as well as imported teas are usually available in cafes and restaurants.

Taza Cup.

Trago Drink.

Trago Largo A long drink, usually fruit juice based, with or without alcohol.

Vaso Glass without stem. i.e., *vaso de agua*.

Vino patero A home-style wine of the Northwest, named because the white or red grapes are crushed with the feet of the pro-ducers to extract the juice. Rubber boots are used in the Calchaquíes valley. The fermentation process is short, lasting from the harvest in the autumn until the spring, when the wine is considered ready to drink. *Vino patero* is sweet to semi-sweet.

Above—A waiter reading a paper while waiting for customers.
Left—A bandoneón player outside at one of the restaurants in La Boca, Buenos Aires

Eating Out

Where People Eat

Bars, Pubs, Confiterías and Cafés These terms are used for various establishments that serve some type of food and drink but do not offer the full service of a restaurant. Like anywhere else, they can vary greatly with regard to price, service and general comfort. A good deal of Buenos Aires social life is conducted in them. "Meet me at the confitería" is a frequent invitation. **Confitería** is the local term for a cafe, although this term is widely used as well. In general terms, a *café* concentrates on coffee and drinks more than on edibles compared with the confitería.

Pubs are a more modern occurrence and are basically cafes or configures

Above and left—Diners enjoying Sunday lunch at different locations in Buenos Aires.

attempting to imitate Irish or English namesakes; they will offer a wider range of beers than a café or confitería. **Bars** are now almost exclusively confined to hotels and restaurants, although some nostalgic cafes still use the name. Confusing, right?

Almost all of these establishments serve, to a greater or lesser extent, edibles. Indeed many confiterías turn themselves into restaurants at mid-day, offering simple but frequently very good meals. It is considered quite correct to order a simple espresso coffee at any time (unless lunch is being served) and sit as long as one likes, chatting, reading a newspaper or writing a novel. At one time, confiterías were popular tea-houses as well. Today only a few still preserve the tradition, although a pot of tea is always available. (See "Bars and Confiterías" on page 81.)

There are certain customs as to what will be served with a beverage. With a cup of coffee or tea, expect to receive a small sweet pastry or chocolate and a glass of water, slightly gassy. With a beer, soda or mixed drink, usually a small container of a salty snack, such as potato chips or peanuts, will be provided. However, for some reason, seldom is anything provided to accompany a glass of wine. Therefore do not be surprised to find that if one person orders a beer with lunch and the other a glass of wine, the beer is served with a portion of peanuts but nothing accompanies the glass of wine.

Parrilla In a restaurant identified as a *"parrilla"* the meat is cooked on a grill over wood coals. In some locations, this will be the only way that meat is prepared. In others, more options will be presented on the menu. See "The Asado" on page 85 for what to expect.

Degrees of "Doneness"	
vuelta y vuelta	rare
jugoso	medium rare
en su punto	done
bien cocido	well done

Pulpería *"Pulpería"* may appear as part of a name but there are few true pulperías in business any more. At the end of the 19th Century, these were very important to the social and commercial life in the country and in many city neighborhoods. A pulpería was a combination general store and bar which also provided very basic cooking. Hitches were provided for the horses outside and the gauchos would play *truco* and drink *una cerveza* (or more) while their wives bought supplies.

"Tenedor libre" and *"diente libre"* in a window or sign indicate these are

"All-you-can-eat" restaurants.

Ice Cream Argentines love ice creams and eat them at all times and in all ways. While it is possible to discover the most exotic flavors, those that are most popular worldwide are most popular in Argentina: chocolate, strawberry and vanilla, but there is a difference. Even in the small neighborhood *artesanal heladería*, one's options for chocolate are likely to be nine or more in addition to the simple chocolate. Other flavors with a large popular backing are *sambayon* (*zabaglione*), *dulce de leche*, and *cassata*—a block with three flavors in layers. A Charlotte is a block of vanilla ice cream with a caramel and almond coating, frequently served with hot chocolate sauce. The complete and correct name for this dish is *Charlotte St. Marceau* but is seldom listed as such.

There are three types of ice creams available: the industrial, of which Frigor is a leader with La Montevedeauna running a close second; the semi-industrial or artesanal which has developed into a chain, such as Freddo; and the artesanal, neighborhood shop that can be found almost anywhere, easily identified by the word "*Heladería*" displayed prominently on its sign.

Argentine ice creams are based on Italian methods and traditions and are totally delicious. It is rare to find a below par ice cream. A traditional shop, said to be the first *heladería* in Argentina, is *El Vesubio* at Corrientes 1181, Buenos Aires.

Top—Queuing for ice cream at a heladería on a hot Sunday afternoon.
Left—A café in Recoleta.

Streetside tango in the pedestrian street Florida, Buenos Aires.

Some key terms to know when ordering ice cream:

Bocha Head. One can pay for a *vasito* with one *bocha* but request two flavors.

Canestina A smaller version of a *cestino*.

Cestino An edible wafer basket for containing quantities of ice cream too large to fit into a *cucurucho* or *vasito*.

Cucurucho Ice cream cone with a small pointed end. Slightly greater capacity than a *vasito*.

Vasito Ice cream cone with a flat base.

Tango Shows A very high percentage of visitors and new residents enter through Buenos Aires and a significant number of them will be tempted to view a tango show while there. Since one can choose to go to a show with dinner or to one after dining, logical questions are: What are the trade-offs? Which ones provide a reasonably good meal with a good show?

There are several tango shows that offer reasonably good meals. If you prefer to eat at a restaurant and then attend a tango show, you need to plan to eat earlier than you would if you dine at the show. By choosing to dine at the show, you can linger over your coffee, dessert or after dinner beverage while the show begins. In addition, the larger tango-dinner theaters provide some type of entertainment during the meal, although food service is minimized during the tango show itself to maximize the visitor's enjoyment.

In La Boca, San Telmo, Recoleta and other areas in downtown Buenos Aires, restaurants frequently employ people to hand out advertisements and often there is someone by the door inviting passersby to come in. This is a result of high competition for the many tourists passing by. The quality of these places varies from good to mediocre but they are safe and you do not need to fear being ripped-off by an exorbitant bill.

Chess players in Córdoba

On The Road When seeking out a place to eat while driving on the highway, it is a good idea to keep an eye open for places where a number of trucks are drawn up. Truckers have a good nose for good food at reasonable prices. Avoid bus stops when possible. Do not be put off by a rustic look or be overly tempted into a flashy, modern place. The former is frequently a better deal than the latter. ACA (*Automóvil Club Argentino*) stops are generally safe bets and have the cleanest toilets of all.

Safe Eating and Drinking

In general terms eating and drinking in Argentina is not a risk for visitors. Municipal water in cities and important towns is safe. If in doubt, there is plenty of bottled water available. Food hygiene is also high. Argentina has modern standards of food safety and you should feel comfortable with eating in all but the most humble restaurants, cafes and confiterias. However, there are many illegal food stands set up alongside the roads vending grilled meats. By their very nature these stands are not subjected to food sanitation inspections and should be avoided. Occasionally, in out of the way places, fish and seafood might present a problem, especially if eaten far removed from the sea, river or lake.

Restaurant Protocol

Hours With very few exceptions, Argentine restaurants, even the most exclusive, are less formal than in the U.S. or Europe. Reservations are taken, although even on weekends they may be superfluous in the current economic depression. Reservations are recommended during holiday periods. Expect to be able to linger through your meal and chat over coffee or drinks afterward. Seldom will you be presented with your bill before you ask for it. The customary phrase used is *La cuenta por favor,* or *La adición por favor.* However, the gesture of signing a bill in the air works as well here as in other parts of the world. Should you need to call for your waiter's attention, "*Mozo*" is the word to use, unless your waiter is a woman, in which case it should be "*moza.*" "*Señor*" or "*señora*" works fine as well.

Normal hours for midday lunch are 1 to 3:30 PM and for dinner from 9 PM to 11PM, although restaurants are frequently open for dinner at 8 PM or even earlier in small cities and towns, and in many cases people will not arrive for dinner until 11 PM.

Smoking Smoking and non-smoking areas are common. And although non-smoking areas are frequently infringed and cigar smoking is not always totally prohibited, non-smoking restaurants are beginning to appear.

Wine Service While most maître d's and waiters are well informed as to food, there are still few sommeliers around who deserve the name. If you are a wine buff, refer to our list of recommended brands or develop your own by visiting one of the wine bars and trying a few wines. If you would like to see the wine list, ask for "*la carta de vinos.*"

Tipping A service or cover charge is frequently but not always added to your check (the menu and bill will say something like "*Cubierto.*") but tips or *propinas* are not. A rule of thumb on tipping used by locals is 10% of the total, within maximum and minimum reason. If paying by credit card, most establishments do not have provisions to add a tip to the charge and you will need to leave it in cash.

Complimentary Drinks In better restaurants complimentary drinks—a glass of bubbly or a sherry on arrival, for example—are usual and do not mean that you are expected to order the bottle!

The Menu First of all, an important point for inexperienced international travelers: In Spanish speaking countries, the word "menu" refers to an offering of several courses for a fixed price, such as "*menú del día.*" In the discussion below, menu is used in the English context, as a list of all of the dishes available.

Many menus attempt to be bilingual, both Spanish-English and Spanish-French. Results range from useful to hilarious or incomprehensible. Would

you order, for example, a dish of "revolting eggs" when you had scrambled eggs in mind? This is but one of innumerable examples which have been noted while reading menus in restaurants. We hope this guide will help you understand what is really being offered.

Holidays and Food

Every country has its own set of holidays and associated with many are traditional foods. Argentina is no different. As Christmas approaches, the stores start to fill with many of the same food items found at the Christmas season in Europe despite it being winter there and summer in Argentina. Stollens, English Puddings, Panettones, candies, dried fruits, nuts, a wider range of cheeses and many other items typical of European countries are common. The mix between products

Las Violetas customers next to the pastry display.

imported or made in Argentina by descendents of European immigrants is a function of the economy. During *Semana Santa* or Holy Week, which is the end of Lent, seafood is traditionally eaten and it is more widely available in supermarkets, with larger than normal fish as are appropriate for special occasions. Otherwise, an asado is the traditional meal for all gatherings, whether for holidays or special events such as a birthday. The foods served also vary with the ethnic background of the family.

Common Errors

Many English speaking, non-Spanish fluent, visitors misread or misunderstand some common words. Here are some tips to help. *"Hoy"* means today. It is often used to indicate today's special on signs outside of restaurants and stores. *"Hay"* means "it exists, there are," and is used on signs in much the same way that *"Hoy"* is. Thus, *"Hay pizza"* does not indicate that they are selling pizzas for horses but that today they have pizzas. Another error is to forget that *"tostado"* is the shorthand for a toasted ham and cheese sandwich. If you want toast and jam you should ask for *pan tostado con mermelada* to ensure you are not misunderstood..

Below—Seals on the rocky shore of an island in the Beagle Channel, Ushuaia.

Places to Eat

Below is a limited selection of places to eat in Buenos Aires and throughout Argentina.

Buenos Aires

Bars and Confiterías

The following selection of bars and confiterías in Buenos Aires have proven popular over the years and can be expected to continue to be so. They are truly classics.

Clasica y Moderna *Callao 892.* Founded in 1958, this marvelous combination of bookshop, snackbar and café is unique in the city. Drop in for a coffee or light snack at midday and emerge with a book autographed by an author who happened to be seated at the table next to yours.

Confitería Ideal *Suipacha 384.* In the heart of the movie and theater district, this is a legendary meeting place for tea, while enjoying a slice of Argentina's Art-Nouveau past. In the late afternoons live music, usually an organ-

One of the stained glass windows in Las Violetas.

ist, provides memories of the past with old favorites.

Las Violetas *At the corner of Avenue Rivadavia and Medrano.* This classic *confitería*, inaugurated in 1884, closed in June 1998 and was immediately declared a site of historic interest. Restored to its original condition, it reopened April 2001. It is well worth a taxi or metro ride to visit. Take a book to read or postcards to write and relax at one of the many tables, enjoying the stained glass windows, food and drinks in a relaxing ambience. If you like sweets, it will take some time to get past the pastry section.

The Tortoni, one of the traditional cafes of Buenos Aires.

Tortoni *Avenida de Mayo and Maipu.* The oldest of Buenos Aires' traditional bars (founded 1858), this center of musical and literary life is a must visit to be made at least once. While no longer the center of the city's cultural life, Tortoni still attracts leading figures from literary, musical, artistic and political circles.

Criolla Restaurants

(Empanadas, carbonadas, and regional foods)

La Cupertina Cabrera 5296; 4777-3711

El Sanjuanino Posadas 1515; 4802-2909

Parilla *(Barbecues)*

La Brigada Estados Unidos 465; 4361-5557. Best of the typical parrillas.

Cabaña Las Lilas Av. Alicia Moreau de Julio 516; 4313-1336. The most elegant parilla.

La Raya Ortiz de Ocampo 2566; 4802-5763

Seafood Restaurants

Parolaccia de Mare Baez 292; 4778-0399

Sapore di Mare San Martin 774; 4312-8577

Italo-Argentine Restaurants

Guido's Bar Republica de la India 2843; 4802-2391. Small, informal and very popular.

Lucky Luciano Cerviño 3943; 4802-1262. Just around the corner from and a slightly upscale version of Guido's Bar.

Pierino Lavalle 3499; 4864-5715. Has kept

Regional Empanadas

For the most part, these are for empanada takeout with little more than a counter and stools to eat on premises. However, they also offer other regional dishes such as locro, carbonada, humitas, tamales and regional desserts.

Catamarca **La Cocina** Florida 142, Pueyrredon 1508

Salta **Dona Eulogia** Castex 3425; 4804-9098

Salta **Tatú** Agüero 1978; 4823-1011, S. de la Independencia 1023; 4772-5522

San Juan **Sanjuanino** Posadas 1515

Tucumán **La Cupertina** Cabrera 5300 at Godoy Cruz; 4777-3711

Tucumán **La Querencia** Esmeralda 1392; Junin 1304; 4827-9477/1802

Tucumán **El Federal** Honduras 5251; 4832-5000

Arab style **Angelina** Cordoba 5270

Arab style **Sarkis** Thames 1101; 4772-4911

Italo-Argentines happy since 1906.

Filo San Martin 975; 4311-0312. Venetian cuisine plus pizza and a crazy mix of art and music.

Traditional Restaurants "Porteño"

1880 Defensa 1665, at Park Lezama. Traditional cooking, in a house built in 1880. Near Plaza Dorrego.

Chiquin Gral J. D. Peron 920; 4327-1066. A classic since 1906.

El Palacio de la Papa Frita Corrientes 1612; 4374-8073. Soufflé potatoes and other local favorites.

Ligure Juncal 855; 4393-0644. Since 1933 without a change in menu.

Sabot 25 de Mayo 756; 4313-6587. Low profile, genuine and with the best *panqueque de manzana* in town.

Tango Spectaculars *Places offering dinner and a tango show.*

El Querandí Perú 302. Tel: 4345-0331/1770. URL: http://www.querandi.com.ar. A smaller, more intimate arrangement.

Esquina Carlos Gardel
Located just off Corri-
entes, at the corner of
Carlos Gardel and
Anchorena. Tel: 4867-
6363. URL: http://
www.esquinacarlos-
gardel.com.ar/ Check
out the site to see
where you'd prefer to
sit and how much it
will cost.

Señor Tango Vieytes
1653 and Osvaldo
Cruz. Tel./Fax: 4303-
0231/2/3/4. URL: http:/
/www.turismo.gov.ar/
espect/sr_tango/
home.htm. With a
capacity to feed 1600
people, this is not a
small place and the
show is a big spectacu-
lar.

Restaurant Reviews For
other types of cuisine, traditional, ethnic, etc., as
well as for more informa-
tion on the above, there
are several restaurant
guides in Spanish. Many
are barely disguised pro-
motional efforts, paid for
by the participating restaurants. This is true of all of
the glossy, colourful guides
on sale. Far more reliable
and honest guides are
those prepared by food
critics Vidal Buzzi, Alicia
Delgado and Abel Gonza-
lez. For information in

English, check the restau-
rant column published
Sundays by the Buenos
Aires Herald.

Beyond Buenos Aires

Bariloche *(02944)*

Il Gabbiano Av.
Bustillo Km 24,300;
(02944) 44-8346

Jauja Quaglia 366;
(02944) 42-2952

Kandahar 20 de
Febrero 698; (02944)
42-4702

Córdoba *City*

Novecento Av. Poeta
Lugones 370; (0351)
460-5299

Oxford Buenos Aires
214; (0351) 422-4012

El Calafate

La Tablita Cnel Ros-
ales 28; (02902) 49-
1065

La Cocina Av. del Lib-
ertador 1245; (02902)
49-1758

Mar del Plata

El Viejo Pop Centro
Comercial Puerto,
Local 7; (0223) 480-
0147

Pepe Nero Cordoba Corner Avellaneda; (0223) 494-9854

___

Mendoza *City*

___

1884 Belgrano 1188, Godoy Cruz—Part of Escorihuela winery, owned by renown chief Francis Mallman; (0261) 424-2698

Bistro M. In Park Hyatt Hotel, Chile 1124; (0261) 441-1200

Don Mario 25 de Mayo 1324; (0261) 431-0810

El Retortuño Dorrego 173 (Guaymallén); (0261) 431- 6300

___

Puerto Iguazú

___

Sheraton Iguazú Resort (03757); 49-1810

Iguazú Grand Hotel (03757); 49-8050

___

Puerto Madryn

___

Centro de Pescadores Artesenales Bv. Brown, 7th rotunda.

El Chalet Humphreys 123 (corner with Thomas). (02965) 454-900

___

Salta *City*

___

El Solar del Convento Caseros 444; (0387) 421-5124

Lo de Andrés Juan Carlos Dávalos at Gorriti, San Lorenzo; (0387) 492-1600

Peña Balderrama San Martin 1126; (0387) 421-0915

___

Ushuaia

___

Tia Elvira Av. Maipu 349; (02901) 424-725

Kaupe Roca 470; (02901) 422-704

The Asado

There are many ways to prepare an asado. The generic term asado literally means roast or (less frequently) grill and the central ingredient is (almost) always some kind of meat or flesh. There are two basic methods used in preparing an asado:

A la parilla (a barbecue). See picture next page.

Al spiedo (spit)—also referred to as *"parrilla vertical"* or *"a la cruz."* See page 31.

The first is the most common, especially for beef, while the second is more usual when roasting lamb and kid. At home, an Argentine asado is always cooked with the heat from wood coals. No self respecting Argentine would use a gas grill and if

A typical home parrilla.

he was forced to use charcoal briquets, he would check to ensure that his neighbors were not looking. Those who have immigrated to the U.S. and have adopted gas grills, are considered traitors to their culture.

The type of meats and offal used is extremely varied and is also influenced by the locale. Parilla restaurants in cities and the province of Buenos Aires can vary greatly from what one finds up country and there are additional differences between provinces. Beef, mutton, lamb, pork and kid are the most widely used, but chicken and some kinds of fish are also quite frequently found.

Liver, kidney, tripe, sweetbread and udder are considered almost-essential when one orders a *"parrillada mixta"* (mixed grill). However, there is one constant that makes or breaks a successful asado: the chorizo or sausage. These fall into three main types: the *"chorizo criollo,"* the *"salchicha"* (a thin long sausage) and the *"morcilla,"* a blood sausage. The quality and composition may vary, but some type of sausage is almost mandatory.

What goes with a typical asado? *"Ensalada mixta"* (a salad of lettuce, onion and tomato dressed with vinegar and oil) and empanadas. And, of course, plenty of good red Argentine wine.

If you are invited to an asado at someone's home, thank your lucky stars, dress informally, arrive hungry and be prepared to eat a lot. Typically, empanadas will be offered while the food is cooking. Then, the host will offer *chorizo, morcilla* and possibly sweetbreads or some other offal meats. An *ensalada mixta* as well as other salads and bread will also be available. Then the host will offer a selection of other meats. When you are sure you cannot eat anything else, the hostess will offer one or more desserts to tempt you. An asado at home is a leisurely meal that will last a couple of hours. If you bring a bottle of wine for the host and hostess, do not expect it to be set aside for later. It will be opened and shared during the meal.

Special Requirements

When you arrive at a restaurant, if you have special dietary requirements, let the waiter know what they are and they will let you know if they cannot accommodate you.

Vegetarians

Meat dominates cooking habits in Argentina which creates problems for vegetarians. However, there are a growing number of vegetarians in Argentina and there are vegetarian restaurants in Buenos Aires and several of the larger cities. In addition, there are many sources of organic foods.

Apart from salads, one must choose carefully to avoid items which do not contain meat. Soups are usually based on meat broths, which are often used in preparing rice dishes. When available, grilled vegetables usually share the grill with meats.

Many pastries are made with lard. Foccia, which in Italy is commonly made with olive oil, is frequently made with lard here.

In a restaurant, pasta is normally fresh pasta made with egg. Some menus will

Polo is a popular Argentine sport and it has the best polo players in the world.

Paintings at Cuevas de las Manos, Santa Cruz.

have a section for fresh (*fresca*) pasta and one for dry (*seca*) pasta. If in doubt, ask.

All corn and soy products must be considered as genetically modified (GM).

Pizza dough is fat free and a popular pizza "*fugazza*" is a cheeseless one topped with sweet onions and which can often be bought by the slice.

For more information on vegetarian options, contact:

Unión Vegetariana Argentina (UVA)
http://www.uva.org.ar
email: uva@ivu.org

Gluten-Free Diet

Although bread and pasta are very important in the average Argentine's diet, there are many alternatives. Many Italo-Argentine restaurants, including less fancy ones, offer polenta on the menu. Rice is a common menu item and in the Northeast, manioc plays an important role in the daily diet. Quiñoa is another option, although rarely appearing in restaurant menus. In a pizzeria, look for a fainá, the garbanzo flour version of a pizza. As a rule salads are dressed with oil and wine vinegar. Meats are normally prepared plain, or at most served with an oil based dressing. Although fried seafoods will contain flour, there are plenty of other preparations that do not use it.

Children

The Argentines love children and take theirs to restaurants, so if you are traveling with children do not worry. Although Argentines routinely eat late, there are plenty of options if you want to feed your children earlier. Many restaurants have children's plates and sharing a dish with your children (or between parents) is never a problem. For mothers with small infants, it is acceptable to nurse your baby in public.

Right—The "Floralis Genérica" sculpture, Palermo, Buenos Aires.

Eating In

This section is designed more to address the needs of residents than those of tourists who might wish to buy their own food and prepare meals. However this should result in providing the tourist with more information than they need whereas to focus on the tourist would short-change the more exten-sive needs of residents. In addition, this addresses the problem in terms of Bue-nos Aires where most incoming new residents will be facing the problem of learning how to live and shop in a new country. The details of where to shop in other cities will be different but the principles should be the same.

Shopping

Where to Shop

When one is living in a foreign country, there is a natural tendency to make purchases in a store where one can see and handle the merchandise before making a selection. This helps avoid mistakes when one is not fluent with the

Above—Cured sausages and cheeses on sale at the annual fair in La Rural.
Left—The old Patagonia Express pulling into the sta-tion at Esquel, Chubut.

language. However, it has some real disadvantages. You are literally on your own and have to rely on what you pick up from others to make good deci-sions.

Buying from small shop keepers, such as the neigh-borhood fruit seller, can offer real rewards over the long run. For one, you will never develop a personal relationship with the peo-ple in a supermarket such as Disco, Jumbo or the others. However, it will not take very many repeat visits to a small shop before you will be recognized and asked where you are from, and a personal relationship will start to develop. Shopping in small stores is a linguistic forcing-function that will improve your ability to communicate and will reward you in many other ways.

A good fruit and vegetable vendor will always want to know when you want to eat certain items, such as avocados and melons, that continue to mature after being picked—not all do.

Supermarkets At the top of the heap in more than one way are the supermarkets or "*supermercados*" and hypermarkets. Chains such as Disco, Norte, Jumbo, and Carrefour are large with extensive supplier networks and high turnover of everything. Many of their stores are really hypermarkets selling clothes, appliances and a wide range of non-food items. They have large produce sections where you can select your own fruits and vegetables. Most meat is precut and packaged on their premises. In addition,

they carry the lines of some large firms that prepare and seal cuts of meat for sale under their label, such as La Hacienda, Las Lilas and Aberdeen Angus. This is a convenient and easy way to shop, particularly for those who are uncomfortable with using their Spanish in dealing with a butcher, or who prefer to read package labels.

There are also many small neighborhood independent supermarkets.

Produce (Verdulerías)

Fruits and vegetables can be purchased in the vegetable section of supermarkets or a neighborhood "*verdulería.*" There are verdulerías in *mercados*, such as the one in Belgrano.

However, do not waste your time looking for a farmers market. They do not exist in Buenos Aires. You will also see itinerant vendors selling fruits and vegetables from a truck parked on the street or women who are selling from baskets or boxes on the sidewalk. The latter are illegal, unlicensed retailers, not producers selling directly to the public. You will only find such producer sales at roadside stands out in the provinces well away from the city of Buenos Aires. Because of the current economic situation in Argentina, many of the new items that appeared in local markets during the mid-90s are less readily available.

Butchers (Carniceros) A big advantage of going to a butcher is that you can ask for the cut you want in the size that you want. Most supermarkets, just like those in the States, have a meat counter where you can ask for them to cut something special for you. However, since they cut ahead to set out packaged meat, they may have already used up their day's supply of meat and will not be able to do it for you. To avoid such problems, you will need a real *carnicero*. The best way to find one is to ask neighbors who buy meat locally. Otherwise you need to walk around and check out the ones in your neighborhood to see which ones look good to you. Don't be surprised if the one favored by most local people isn't very modern. If you want something special such as ground pork or veal for that special meatloaf recipe, you will need a *carnicero* to prepare it for you.

A ambulatory garlic vendor with ribboned braids of garlic for Christmas time.

93

Bakeries (Panaderías) etc.

Buying baked goods is rather complicated because there are no commonly agreed-to terms of reference or national standards. The bakers in Buenos Aires represent regional as well as extra-national influences, incorporating the heritage and personal tastes of the baker. Therefore you may find a French, Italian or European bakery. When the term "European" is used, it means German or Eastern Europe and reflects Austro-Hungarian preferences rather than French styles, which can be quite different. There is also a relatively large Middle-Eastern population in Argentina and thus many bakers reflecting their preferences.

For someone who likes bread and other bakery products, there are lots of choices. It is only a question of finding one convenient for your daily needs and knowing where to go for the especial items required for special occasions. There are panaderías, pastelerías and confiterías. Panaderías and pastelerías specialize in bread and pastries respectively, but a confitería prepares and sells other foods,

A selection of desserts ready to take home.

such as sandwiches, savory pies, baked stuffed peppers, etc.

Cheeses Argentina is a country of immigrants. This has influenced their styles of cheese just as other aspects of their cuisine. Therefore most of the cheeses produced and sold here are characterized by the same names as in their native countries, with in some cases slight changes to the names. Because there are also imported cheeses available, you may find several different cheeses, with those from Argentina (Industria Argentina) displayed side by side with those from other countries. You need to make a selection based on price and personal preference. But you should try the local version because most are quite good.

Pasta A very happy result of all of the Italian immigrants to Argentina is the availability of stores that deal primarily in fresh pasta. You can eat fresh pasta with very little effort. You can even order by phone and have it delivered! Select the number of canelones with the filling you desire and pick a sauce or a combination of sauces. Mix or match. All provide take-home listings of what they sell. Pick up one and study it. The possibilities are so many that you need time to make a selection.

Home delivery, Buenos Aires style.

A typical refrigerated display of fresh pasta.

Home Delivery Before you start going shopping, you may note one sign of a Buenos Aires phenomena, home delivery, when you see the young men from Disco pushing their stacked delivery baskets through the neighborhood. Almost every business advertises that it will *envío*—deliver—its products. The businesses that do this range from supermarkets to pasta stores to ice cream shops to restaurants. This is a relatively new development; old timers say that it has increased considerably in the past five years. Many businesses allow internet orders for home delivery. For some of the supermarkets, there is a minimum purchase for free delivery. You need to know the minimum before you walk in and make an inexpensive but heavy purchase, expecting to have it delivered but being told "no" because it is under their

95

Honey on tap at a health food store.

minimum. Even if you do not expect to use home delivery often, you should give it a try before you need this service so you know how it works.

Whenever you are in a store which you feel you might wish to revisit or order items from, ask for a *tarjeta*. They will probably give you an *imán*, a magnetized version of a business card to place on your refrigerator. Remember to ask for a *lista de productos* if appropriate. This will give you a list of items and prices. The process is like ordering pizza from home except it is for other food items or products. Thus armed, and having tried it out, you are ready for the rainy day when the kids are cranky and you really don't want to go out but need to feed them.

Shopping for Special Items

Knowing the Argentine names of what you want is only part of the problem. Several items frequently used in contemporary U.S. and European cooking have not been widely adopted here. In addition, there are always people who have special dietary needs. Here are a few places you need to know about.

✔**Mercado de Belgrano** The Mercado in Belgrano is located on Juramento between Cuidad de Paz and Amenabar. It is open 8 AM to 1 PM and 5 PM to 8:30 PM Monday through Saturday. During the Christmas holiday season it stays open longer. Inside are many permanent shops selling all types of meats, seafood, cheeses, pasta, fruits and vegetables and other items. You owe it to yourself to make a visit.

★ Mercado de San Telmo

This is truly one of the old time markets. Located near Plaza Dorrego, it is in the center of the block bounded by Defensa, Bolívar, Carlos Calvo and Estados Unidos with an entrance from each. This is the most accessible market for tourists.

Chinatown In Belgrano, primarily along Arribeñas between Juramento and Olazábal, is a small area with many Chinese restaurants and shops, including small supermarkets. If you like to prepare meals using oriental ingredients, here is a must place to shop. These supermarkets are also a great place to look for spices, unusual mixes, special teas and serendipity.

Health Food Stores There are many health food stores in Buenos Aires. These are good places to buy organic foods beyond the limited selection available in the large supermarkets. They also have spices and herbs not available in supermarkets. Even if you do not consider yourself a "health-food person," take a look at what they offer.

These stores carry such items as vanilla bean, quiñoa and wild rice. Many also sell honey in bulk. Three from among the many are:

Dietética Obligado.
Belgrano. Vuelta de Obligado 1913

Oro Verde.
Palermo. Santa María de Oro 2568

Dietética Viamonte
Centro. Viamonte 859

Some Others The following are good places to try but are hard to classify. El Gato Negro, for example, is a café/bar/restaurant that sells a wide variety of spices, teas and coffees downstairs. It has five different types of curry powders. Casa Polti, located next to the Belgrano Mercado, has a wide variety of spices, sweets, and real, versus artificial, vanilla extract for sale. It has the other also, so you need to ask. It also carries baking chocolate.

El Gato Negro
Centro. Corrientes 1669

Casa Polti
Belgrano. Juramento 2499

Mercado Central Buenos Aires has a *Mercado Central*, or Central Market, located at Autopista Ricchieri (the autopista to Ezeiza) and Boulogne Sur Mer, the first interchange after the *peaje*. The Mercado Central opens early—very early for the wholesale crowd—and closes in the late afternoon. This is where you can find out-of-season and exotic fruits and vegetables and many other things. It can be intimidating because it is so large. Remember, the produce for a city of several million people moves through the Mercado Central.

Measures

Argentina uses the metric system in all of its weights and measures. Food is sold in grams and kilos for loose goods and in liters for liquids with few exceptions. For conversions, see "Conversion of Metric & English Units" on page 124.

Mineral Content	
Calcio	Calcium
Magnesio	Magnesium
Sodio	Sodium
Potasio	Potassium
Cloruro	Chlorine
Bicarbonato	Bicarbonate
Sulfato	Sulfates
Nitratos	Nitrates
Total Solidos disueltos	Total dissolved solids

Rules of Thumb Although a purist might point out that 1 kilogram equals 2.2047 lbs., a useful rule of thumb when making purchases is that 1/2 kilo roughly equals a pound. If you want about a pound of something, it is sufficient to say *"Un medio kilo de..."* That is a lot easier than trying to ask for 450 grams (or to be more precise 453.6 grams). Use *un cuarto kilo* for half a pound. A

Below—Bags of "Zapallo" and onions in the Mercado Central.
Right—A fish display in the Mercado de Belgrano.

quart is roughly equal to a liter (0.9463L).

Product Labels

All packaged goods are obliged to show the amount of the contents on the package label. Bottled water containers indicate the mineral content. In the case of perishables such as milk, the expiration date must be clearly marked. This has been extended to almost all goods including such items as dish washing detergent.

In addition, for processed food, you will find content information (e.g., % of fat *grasa*), in a format consistent with standard international usage. There is no requirement to indicate genetically modified products.

Meat cuts will be labeled with the kind and cut of meat, date, price per kilo, weight and total price. For more detailed information, see "Meat Cuts and Labeling" on page 117.

Organic Products

Argentina has laws and regulations governing the production, certification and labeling of organic products. To be labeled organic, the products must be grown or raised without using chemical fertilizers, pesticides, artificial hormones or genetically modified materials.

Buying Fish and Meat

This section is much longer than would be expected in a tourist guide because it is also designed to meet the needs of non-native residents. Argentines are beef eaters, which is why so much attention and emphasis is placed on anything concerning meat. Lately lamb has begun to grow in favor, while pork and kid trail behind. Poultry and fish are not considered true meats, although consumption of fish is slowly increasing.

Beef

Cattle-Raising Differences

In the U.S., all cattle start out eating grass; three fourths of them are finished (grown to maturity) in feedlots where they are fed specially formulated feed based on corn or other grains. This adds weight and fat to the cat-

tle. Cattle raising practices in many other countries are similar. Until recently, Argentine cattle were all grass-fed and there were very few feedlots in Argentina and these were for the export market. A recent development is increased use of feedlots although this is still only a small portion of Argentine beef. A grass-fed cow is leaner and lighter when it goes to slaughter. Once slaughtered, Argentine beef is matured in the same way as in the U.S., on a grappling hook in controlled conditions for between one day and a week, with Argentine practice favoring the shorter period. During this maturation period, enzymes naturally occurring in the cow's body undertake a process that breaks down certain meat fibers, resulting in a more tender meat. Aging requires storage under controlled conditions and thus "aged beef" is more expensive.

Beef Categories Generally speaking, world-wide practice is to categorize

Date Labeling	
Fecha de Vencimiento (VEN)	Expiration Date
Fecha Evase (ENV)	Date Packaged
Fecha Elaboración (ELAB)	Date Manufactured

A typical parilla with Pamplonas, red peppers, a steak, chorizo, morcilla, cordero, and tira de asado.

meat, particularly beef, by the age of the animal. In Argentina the three terms commonly used for beef are: *Ternera*, *Novillo* and *Vaca*. *Ternera* is the youngest, tenderest and most expensive with *vaca* the oldest, toughest and cheapest. Ternera is young beef weighing up to 73 kilos dressed. Novillo is a steer. You may also encounter *vaquillona* (heifer) and *novillito* (young steer). In addition, although you may see reference to *mamón* in some old Spanish cookbooks you will never encounter it on the Argentine market. *Mamón* is the young milk-fed animal up to about 50 kilos dressed. By Argentine law, animals which are still nursing cannot be slaughtered, thus there is no *mamón* available on the Argentine market.

For comparison, in the U.S., "Beef" is used for cattle about 2 years old which weigh about 1000 lbs. (450 Kg.) on the hoof. "Baby Beef" and "Calf" are used for younger cattle, weighing about 700 lbs. (345 Kg.). Veal is meat from a calf normally weighing about 150 lbs (74 Kg.). Under USDA grading standards, the difference between calf and veal is based on the color of the meat. Veal is pale pink. Argentine cattle sold as ternera are always older and the meat is redder than U.S., British or French veal although most books translate *"ternera"* as "veal."

Common Beef Cuts *Milanesas* are very popular in Argentina. They are very thin cuts of meat, normally beef, that are

101

breaded when cooked. Milanesas come from several different primary cuts of meat and the packages are marked to indicate which, such as *milanesa de nalga*.

Bife de Chorizo is usually a very thick cut and is boneless. *Bife Angosto* is similar to a New York strip with the bone and cut thinner. It is usually somewhat cheaper.

The terms *bife* and *churrasco* are fairly interchangeable and mean a slice of meat, usually one to two inches thick. A *churrasco* is always boneless.

For a complete listing of cuts of beef, see "Packaged Beef" on page 117.

Sausages There are three Argentine words in "Packaged Pork" on page 121 which translate into "sausage," and there are additional variations. Argentine sausages are very different from an American or British breakfast sausage. They contain much less fat and do not cook down as much. The Argentine "*chorizo*" is also very different from a Mexican "*chorizo*," with none of the expected spices. Argentine *chorizos* are fat link sausages while the *loganiza* is thinner and usually

sold as one long piece for the buyer to cut into smaller ones. *Salchicha* is casually used; sometimes to refer to something similar to a hot dog or long vienna sausage in taste and texture but sometimes applied to thin link sausages which are more closely akin to a chorizo. It is very difficult to find anything in a *carniceria* that corresponds to what is marketed in the U.S. as Italian or Polish sausages.

Poultry

Poultry can be bought in supermarkets or *carnicerias*. However there are a few special stores, usually found as part of a mercado that specialize in poultry and other farm products. They will have *granja* (farm) as part of their name or prominently displayed as part of their sign. In these shops you can find a variety of meats from farm-raised animals: chickens, turkeys, ducks, geese, rabbits, partridge, quail, pheasant, deer and whatever else depending on the owner.

Argentine chickens are large and usually have a lot of fat under the skin. There are several types or grades of chickens sold.

Most packaged chickens sold are raised in industrialized facilities, using hormones, similar to the U.S. There are two other types, similar to U.S. *free range* chickens. Of these, those labeled as *ecologico* are fed organically raised feed and cost more as a result. *"De campo"* corresponds to what people in the U.S. refer to as free range.

75% of the turkeys sold in Argentina come from Brazil. Most of the rest come from Chile. For special meals you can try cooking a pheasant, which is smaller than a turkey and not difficult to prepare. Sometimes available in supermarkets is *magret de pato*, which can be grilled as a delightful alternative to beef. For additional information, see "Poultry" on page 123.

Fish

Argentines are not big fish eaters although Argentina has an abundant supply along its immense Atlantic coast, most of which is exported to Europe and Asia. The most popular sea fish is the *merluza*. *Abadejo* (pollack), *atún* (tuna), *corvina* (croaker), *mero* (grouper) and *pejerrey (de mar)* are also widely eaten.

There are a number of excellent fresh-water and river fish as well. The most popular are the pejerrey and the dorado. These are more difficult to find at the fish mongers but are worth seeking out.

Recipes

The following recipes are provided as examples of typical Argentine cooking. In them, Tbs. is the abbreviation for tablespoon and tsp. is that for teaspoon. If you wish to try out one of the recipes you see in the papers, or you wish to follow the instructions on a package, the following are the key measures and their equivalents:

Measurement Terms	
a gusto	to taste
cucharada	tablespoon
cucharadita	teaspoon
dedalito	thimble (1/2 teaspoon)
entero	whole
medio, al	in half
pizca	pinch
puñado	handful
tacita	small cup (1/2 cup)
taza	cup (8 oz.)
tiritas	strips

Mar Del Plata cocktail

Drinks

MAR DEL PLATA

Enzo Antonetti won the 1964 International Barmans Association World Cocktail Championship with this aperitif.

40 gr. dry Gin
30 gr. dry Vermouth
10 gr. Benedictine
A dash of Gran Marnier

Mix with ice cubes to chill. Strain into a martini glass. Serve with a light squeeze of fresh lemon peel.

LICOR MAPUCHE

Licor Mapuche is a cure for aches and pains and a general restorative of spirits. Following the steps as prescribed is the secret of its effectiveness. "Petty"

Nauta of Estancia Telken attributes this recipe to Pedro Romaniuk.

4 green walnuts cut into slices
1/2 L alcohol (white brandy)

Place nuts in alcohol and let stand for seven days. Pour off alcohol into a 3 liter capacity demijohn.

Pour 1/2 L alcohol over the same nuts and let stand for 14 days. Pour off alcohol into demijohn.

Add another 1/2 L alcohol to nuts and let stand for 21 days. Pour off alcohol into demijohn and throw away the nuts.

Make a syrup with 1/2 L water and 7 Tbs (heaped) of sugar. Cook until fairly thick and concentrated. Let cool and add to demijohn. Add 1 L. Mistela or other darkish sweet white wine. Let stand for 40 days.

Salsas, Marinadas and Adobos

While adobos and marinades are very similar and almost interchangeable, there are a few differences. An adobo is usually rubbed into or placed on the food before cooking (oven, roasting or grilling). A marinada is a mixture, usually quite liquid, in which food is cooked either cold (cerviche) or hot (escabeche). The food is left in the marinade until eaten.

ADOBO DE ACEITE Y AJO

Oil and garlic Marinade

2 Tbs. oil
1/2 clove of garlic, finely
  minced
1 tsp. salt

Mix these ingredients, either in a blender or by hand.

One of the following may also be added: 1/2 teaspoon of one or two of the following (*if using more than two, do not let the total quantity exceed 1 teaspoon.*): chopped parsley, oregano, rosemary, thyme, ground cumin, paprika, crushed red pepper, or cayenne. This marinade is used mainly on chicken or fish.

ADOBO DE ACEITE Y HIERBAS

Oil and Herbs Marinade

2 Tbs. oil
1 tsp. salt
1/2 tsp. freshly ground
  black pepper
2 tsp. of one of the following: finely chopped parsley, chopped oregano

leaves, chopped rosemary leaves

Mix ingredients and use on red meats. Combinations are possible, but not recommended.

ESCABECHE

2 Tbs. oil
1 Tbs. chopped onion
1 Tbs. chopped parsley
1 Tbs. chopped red pepper
1 bay leaf
1 garlic clove, peeled and
  chopped
1 pinch oregano
2 Tbs. vinegar
1 tsp. paprika

Heat oil over moderate heat. Add other ingredients. After a few minutes remove from heat and add vinegar and paprika. Pour over just barely cooked fish or chicken. Let cool, cover and store overnight in refrigerator. Serve cool.

SALSA CRIOLLA

Creole Sauce

There are many variations to this basic sauce, but this is a typical mild version.

1/2 cup oil
1 medium onion, chopped

1 tomato, chopped
1 medium sweet pepper, chopped
1 garlic clove, peeled and bruised
1/2 tps. sweet paprika (*pimentón dulce*)
1/2 tps. cumin (*comino*)
1/2 tps. oregano
—salt to taste

Heat oil. Add onion and heat through. Add tomato, sweet pepper, and garlic. Stir. Add the rest of the ingredients and cook over high heat 3-4 minutes. Serve hot.

Increase quantities if you wish to keep in a jar in the refrigerator for ready use. A "hot" version can be made by adding a teaspoon of chili or cayenne pepper.

CHIMICHURI

10 cloves garlic
1 tsp. oregano
4 bay leaves
2 tsp. sweet paprika
1 tsp. thyme
1 tsp. basil
1 Tbs. chopped parsley
1 tsp. salt
1/2 tsp. ground pepper
1/2 cup oil
1/4 cup vinegar
1 cup boiling water

Mash or finely chop garlic. Mix with other dry ingredients. Place in 2 cup (500 cc) bottle. Add oil, vinegar and water. Shake vigorously. Cool and store in refrigerator until it is to be used. Use to brush meats before and while being grilled and as a sauce to accompany them when served.

Starters

MATAMBRE RELLENO A LA CRIOLLA

Stuffed Flank Steak Criollo

1 large, tender flank steak, about 2 pounds, trimmed and without excess fat
– a little oil
1/2 cup stale bread, diced
1/2 cup hot milk
1 slightly beaten egg
1 slice bacon, in thin strips
1 Tbs. chopped garlic and parsley mixture
1 tsp. oregano
1/2 cup boiled and lightly mashed carrots
1/2 cup drained peas
2 Tbs. grated cheese
– salt and nutmeg to taste
1 sweet red pepper, seeded and peeled, in strips
2 cups creole tomato sauce

Rub into steak a little oil, salt and pepper and let stand 15 minutes. Soak the bread in the milk. Mix the bread cubes, milk, egg, bacon, garlic-parsley mixture, oregano, carrots, peas, and grated cheese together; and season with the salt and nutmeg. Lay meat on a board, lean side upwards, and spread mixture evenly over it. See that the spread is kept about 2 cm (3/4 inch) from the borders, so that it will not ooze out while rolling. Scatter red pepper strips all over the filling.

Roll and tie steak. Place in a shallow roasting pan and roast in a hot oven about ten minutes for it to brown. Lower heat to moderate and continue roasting until tender, about 1-1/2 hours. If serving hot, add tomato sauce and cook 30 minutes more, basting roast with sauce. Serve hot, slicing roast at the table, with a potato salad, mayonnaise and parsley dressing or with a tomato, onion, cauliflower salad or other vegetables.

If serving cold, instead of adding tomato sauce, remove from oven, let cool, then refrigerate until ready to serve. Cut with a sharp knife into finger width slices and place on a serving platter.

ENSALADA MIXTA

Mixed Salad
An Argentine favorite.

To fresh whole lettuce leaves, add sliced tomato and onion. Dress with a vinaigrette of three parts oil and one part vinegar. Salt to taste. Toss and serve.

SALPICÓN DE AVE

Chicken Salpicón
In Argentina, a salpicón means a vegetable salad to which some red or white meat has been added, dressed with a simple mayonnaise and served cold or at room temperature.

Use cubed boiled chicken meat or cubed leftover roast chicken meat., dressing it with mayonnaise and pickle mix. Argentines use only unspiced pickles made with a brine and white vinegar mixture. Small pickled cucumbers and cauliflower florets are preferred with an addition of carrots, turnips and celery. Add to the cubed and dressed chicken some boiled white rice, cubed boiled carrots, fresh onion in very thin strips, tomatoes in small cubes of wedges, a little celery or fennel in small dice, oregano and a trace of white ground pepper.

It is served at room temperature. There are no set rules that might limit the possible additions that may be made to any salpicón, so the cook is free to express creativity and use what is available in the market.

ENSALADA RUSA

Russian Salad

This popular salad is found everywhere in Argentina. It is the side dish accompanying most cold meat preparations. This is the traditional recipe. In modern practice, it is seldom made with beets or sweet potatoes.

1 cup boiled potatoes
1 cup boiled carrots
1 cup boiled sweet potatoes
1 cup boiled beets
1 cup boiled/steamed peas
3 Tbs. of mayonnaise

Cut the potatoes, carrots, sweet potatoes and beets in small cubes, almost pea size. Mix all of the vegetables, dress with mayonnaise and serve.

BUDÍN DE CHOCLO AL CARAMELO

Corn Pudding in Caramel

Dating from Argentina's colonial days, this first course is sure to please your guests. Called a pudding, it is more akin to a souffle.

50 grs. butter
1 large onion, chopped
2 cans creamed corn
5 whole eggs, beaten softly
100 g grated cheese
—salt, pepper and a little sugar

Cook the onion in the butter slowly until the onion softens and becomes clear. Add the corn after the pan is removed from the heat. Add the eggs, cheese, salt, pepper, and sugar, blending well. Pour into a previously caramelized souffle dish and bake in a *bain-marie* in a hot oven for about 1 hour, or until set. Remove from the oven, let cool slightly and serve.

Main Courses

PUCHERO

Beef Pot

1 kg lean and tender boiling
  beef
200 grs. salted bacon
1 onion
1 sweet green pepper
1 small bunch parsley
2 medium potatoes, peeled,
  in halves
4 medium carrots,
  scrapped, in halves
4 small tender turnips,
  scraped
2 small sweet potatoes,
  peeled, in halves
--coarse salt, whole pepper-
  corns

Bring to boil, in a large
pot, 3 liters of water with a
little coarse salt. Meanwhile
trim beef, removing excess
fat and tendons. Some may
wish to quarter the meat to
help it cook more rapidly,
especially if it is a less tender
cut. Prepare vegetables. As
soon as the water begins to
boil, add the beef and all
vegetables at once. Bring
back to a boil over high
heat. Maintain the high boiling pace for about an hour,
or a little more, until the
meat is tender.

Remove the meat and
vegetables and keep hot
while making a soup with
the broth by adding any
pastina, italian soup
noodles, semolina, or any
quick cooking starch. Serve
soup first, when ready. later,
serve puchero, the meat in
one dish and the vegetables
in another. Everything must
be taken to the table piping
hot. Salt, vinegar and oil
accompany all pucheros at
the table as well as other
condiments, such as
prepared mustard. In
addition, other quick
cooking ingredients may be
added to taste, meat or
vegetable. Cut link sausage,
zucchini, leeks, squash and
fresh ears of corn are among
the most widely used ones.

PASTEL DE PAPAS

Shepherd's Pie

4 cups mashed potatoes,
  seasoned with butter and
  salt
2 eggs
1 tsp. chopped parsley
2 Tbs. grated cheese
1 medium onion, chopped
2 tomatoes, chopped
1 Tbs. tomato extract
1 garlic clove, minced
1 sweet pepper, in strips
1/2 cup oil
2 cups ground beef
—salt and pepper to taste

Heat oil and fry onion with garlic, add sweet peppers and then stirring all the time, add tomatoes and tomato extract and cook over a quick fire for a few minutes until the tomatoes are cooked and soft. Add ground beef, stirring to blend all ingredients well. When beef changes color, season, remove from heat and let stand for five minutes.

Mix and blend well the mashed potatoes, eggs, parsley and cheese. Oil a baking dish and spread half of the potato mixture evenly on the bottom. Lay the ground beef preparation over the mashed potatoes, spreading the mixture evenly, and cover with the rest of the mashed potatoes. Score the top with the tines of the fork and bake in a moderate oven until the top is lightly browned. Serve hot.

BIFES A LA CRIOLLA

Criollo Potted Steak

1 kg lean beef, sliced in thin strips
2 Tbs. simple garlic and oil dressing (oil, minced garlic, chopped parsley and salt)
—lemon juice or vinegar

1/2 cup oil
2 large onions, cut in not too thin rounds
2 large sweet peppers, red or green in thin strips
2 large tomatoes, cut in thin wedges
1 tsp. chopped parsley
1 bay leaf
1/2 cup beef broth or stock, or boiling water
—salt and pepper to taste

Have beef cut into very thin steaks, pound them to flatten evenly, and let stand for 15 minutes in a simple oil, salt, chopped garlic and parsley dressing rubbed thoroughly into the steaks; add a few drops lemon juice or vinegar. (See "Adobo de Aceite y Hierbas" on page 105 for correct proportions.)

Drain steaks, pour remaining dressing into a large iron casserole with a cover, heat oil but do not let it sizzle. Put onion rings on bottom, set steaks on onions, flatten, cover with tomatoes and peppers, parsley and broth. Season with bay leaf, salt and a little ground black pepper, and let simmer for about an hour, or until steaks are very tender. As a general rule, the cut of meat selected for this dish is not necessarily very tender. Serve hot. It requires no additional accompaniments except for a green salad.

Desolved

Desserts

AMBROSÍA

Ambrosia

An ambrosia is an egg preparation with syrup which offers many variations with the addition of dried fruit, liquors, juices, and pureed fruits. This version uses orange juice.

1 Tbs cornstarch, well rounded
2 cups sugar
1 1/2 cups boiling water
2 whole eggs beaten with
2 egg yolks
4 Tbs fresh orange juice, strained
—pinch grated nutmeg or vanilla to taste

In a small sauce pan, mix the sugar and cornstarch, stirring to ensure that ingredients are well blended to avoid lumps. While continuing to stir, add boiling water and bring to a boil over low heat. Cook 3 minutes. Beat the eggs and egg yolks, orange juice and nutmeg or vanilla. Remove the cornstarch preparation from the heat, and stirring vigorously gradually pour in beaten egg mixture. Return to the

heat and simmer gently two more minutes.

Serve cold in stemmed glasses with honey biscuits and sprinkled with chopped nuts.

BUDÍN DE PAN

Bread Pudding

A very popular dessert which has many variations. It can be made over an open fire in a water-bath (bain-marie), steamed, or baked in the oven with or without a bain-marie. This version is made in the oven with a bain-marie so that it will be dryer and lighter.

2 cups stale white bread cut in cubes
2 cups hot milk
3 Tbs. sugar
3 eggs, beaten
—pinch of salt, grated lemon rind or vanilla essence
—seedless raisins to taste

Heat milk to point of boiling. Pour hot milk over bread cubes, soak them well and stir with a fork until well mashed and reduced to shreds. Beat eggs lightly with sugar and a pinch of salt (eggs must not build up any foam), and blend into bread and milk mixture, add raisins in the desired amount and grated lemon rind or vanilla. Pour into a previously caramelized fluted mold and bake in a very slow oven for about 1 hour, or until set. It may also be baked in a *bain-marie*, covered, in a moderate oven, for 45 minutes.

Remove from the oven, let cool completely, loosen around the edges and unmold. Do not attempt to unmold still warm, much less when hot, because it won't hold its shape. Serve cold, plain or with a caramel sauce.

Beat eggs and egg yolks with vanilla and set aside. Bring milk and sugar to a boil. Simmer while stirring with a wooden spoon until the sugar is dissolved. Pour milk into eggs, stirring well. Strain and pour into a previously caramelized custard molds. Place molds into a bain-marie and cook in a medium oven about an hour or until set (when a knife introduced in the custard comes out clean).

FLAN

1 L milk
3/4 cup sugar
4 eggs
2 egg yolks
—vanilla essence

Right—Inside the beach restaurant on the island Mirador del Sol, Rosario, Santa Fe.
Below—Wetlands in Buenos Aires Province.

Additional Information

Contact Information

For information regarding Wine or Food Routes in general, contact:

Secretaria de Agricultura, Granadería, Pesca y Alimentos (SAGPyA)
Av. Paseo Colón 922 Of.163
(1063) Buenos Aires
Email: agrotur@sagpya.
mecon.gov.ar

Secretaría de Turismo de la Nación
Suipacha 1111 piso 21°
(1368) Buenos Aires
www.turismo.gov.ar
Email: turismo@turismo.
gov.ar

For information regarding Wine or Food Routes in Mendoza, contact:

La Fundación Instituto de Desarrollo Rural (IDR)
0261-4292681
fax 0261-4292639
www.idr.org.ar
Email: info@idr.org.ar

The IDR web site is currently only in Spanish but plans are to provide information in English.

Additional Reading

Wineries to visit. Wines to taste—An easy to use bilingual guide to the wine routes of Mendoza; consisting of a packet of 18

Left—Carving servings of lamb at a parrilla.

The authors would appreciate readers comments on errors, omissions, or misleading information.
Email: authors@aromasy
sabores.com

For Updates check:
www.aromasysabores.com

11.5 by 22 cm cards with information and maps. 4953-2603. email: delikatessen@uolsinectis.com.ar

The Gourmet Gaucho—Dereck Foster. Buenos Aires: Emecé, 2001, ISBN 950-04-2257-3. Bilingual sketch of food in Argentina from the arrival of European explorers to the present.

How Argentina Cooks—Alberto Vázquez-Prego. Buenos Aires: El Ateneo, 2000, ISBN 950-02-8349-2. Bilingual recipes.

A baby whale playing in Gulfo Nuevo.

A Brief Lunfardo Glossary

Lunfardo is the name given to the slang language of the people of Buenos Aires, known as Porteños. These include food terms that are used in a different sense.

afanar	to steal	*chorro*	thief
albondiga	totally destroyed	*chorrear*	to steal
		coima	bribe
alcachofa	someone who cannot keep a secret	*coimear*	to bribe
		curda	drunk, tipsy, drunkard
apoliyar	to sleep, snooze	*faso*	fag, cigarette
atorrante	scoundrel	*fiaca*	laziness
bacan	well off	*fideo*	joke
banana	A very intelligent person	*fideos*	hair
		guita	money
bagayo	ugly woman, packet, luggage	*laburar*	to work
		mango	money
Bárbaro!	Very good! Excellent!	*manguear*	to beg, borrow
boludo	stupid, an idiot	*papa*	an adjective meaning beautiful
bondi	bus		
bulin	small apartment (i.e., pad)	*pibe*	boy
		pilchas	clothes
cana	police	*polenta*	vigor
capo	boss	*re*	a prefix added to words for emphasis, meaning very... e.g., "re-consado" means very very tired.
carniza	nickname for butcher		
casata	type of ice-cream, also a very rude word		
changuito	grocery cart.		
(The word arises from the name used to refer to the indigenous men employed to carry packages before there were grocery carts.)		*timba*	betting
		trucho	false, trick
		verde	greenback (dollar)
chirola	coin, small change	*yeta*	bad luck

A bull waits his turn on the auction block at the annual agricultural fair at La Rural in Palermo.

Meat Cuts and Labeling

Introduction to Meat Cuts

The diagrams that follow are approximations, an attempt to represent a three dimensional object in two dimensions. The sources for the information specify the cuts in anatomical terms by bone and muscle. There is some overlay of cuts as the muscles involved overlay each other (e.g., the *nalga* [see page 119], which involves the hindquarter muscles, lies outside of the vacio, part of the diaphragm muscles).

The tenderloin is the same cut in the U.S., UK and France as that for the Argentine *lomo*. Thus it is only depicted in the Argentine diagram. The diagrams show only the principal meat cuts. They are normally further differentiated and labeled.

The listing of cuts starts with the Argentine term in italics *Argentine*, followed by the American term, then the British, and last, the FRENCH.

Packaged Beef Following are the names commonly used on packaged beef you will encounter in supermarkets or *carnicerias*.

Some are special cuts you will only find if you ask for them. Those marked by † are no longer listed by Servicio Nacional de Sanidad y Calidad Agroalimentaria (SENASA) in their guide to the Argentine nomenclature of meats. In spite of this, the public and many

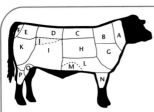

Argentine Beef Cuts *A—Cogote, B—Aguja, C—Bifes anchos, D—Bifes Angostos, E—Cuadril, F—Peceto, G—Carnaza, H—Asado, I—Vacio, J—Lomo, K—Nalga, L—Pecho, M—Falda, N—Brazuelo, O—Bola de Lomo, P—Garrón*

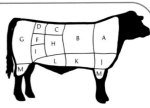

American Beef Cuts A—Chuck, B—Rib, C—Short Loin, D—Sirloin, F—Top Sirloin, G—Round, H—Short Loin, I—Bottom Sirloin, J—Brisket, K—Plate, L—Flank, M—Shank

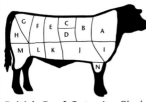

British Beef Cuts A—Clod, B—Blade bone, Chuck, Fore Rib, C—Wing Rib, D—Top Rib, E—Porterhouse steak,, T-bone Steak, Filet, Boneless Sirloin Roast, F—Entrecóte Steak,, Chateaubriand,, Sirloin, Filet, Boneless sirloin roast, Filet Mignon, G—Rump, Rump steak, H—Topside, I—Sticking, J—Brisket, Navel, K—Flank, L—Flank, M—Silverside, Breast N—Shin

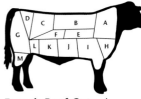

French Beef Cuts *A—COLLIER, PALETRON, B—BASSES CÔTE, C— FILET, ENTRECÓTE, CHATEAUBRIAND, FILET MIGNON, TOURNEDOS, FAUX FILET, CONTRE-FILET, ALOYAU, D—AIGUILLETTE, E—PLAT DE CÔTE, F—PLAT DE CÔTE, CÔTES COUVERTES, ONGLET, G—RUMSTECK, H—POITRINE, I—POITRINE, J—POITRINE, K—HAMPE, L—BAVETTE, M—PLAT DE JARRET, POT AU FEU*

restaurants and parillas freely refer to *bife de chorizo* and *tira de asado*.

Aguja—Chuck, Chuck Roast, Pony 6 ribs, Square cut chuck, BASSES CÔTES, CÔTE COUVERTE

Asado—Short Ribs, Roast Prime Rib, Short Plate, PLATE DE CÔTE

Bife Ancho—Prime Rib, Rib Eye Roast, Rib Eye, Steaks, Spencer Roll, Cuberoll, Rib eye roll, ENTRECÔTE, NOIX D'ENTRECOT

Bife Angosto—Strip Steak, Porterhouse, Steak, Strip Loin, FAUX FILET

Bife a la Rueda—Round (Very large cut, the hind quarter), GLOBE

Bife de Alcatra†—Sirloin Steak

Bife de Costilla—T-Bone Steak

Bife de Chorizo†—Rump Steak

Bife de Vacio—Flank Steak, Flank Steak, BAVETTE, FLANCHE

Bola de Lomo—Sirloin Tip Roast, Thick Flank, Knuckel, TRANCHE GRASSE

Brazuelo—Fore Shank, Fore Shin, JARRET, GITE AVANTE

Carnaza—Stewing Beef, Silverside, Flat, TRANCHE RONDE, TRANCHE SEMELLE, RONDE SEMELLE

Carnaza de Cola—Essentially the same as cuadrada

Carne Picada—Ground Beef

Cogote—Neck, Clod, COLLIER

Colita de Cuadril—Rump Steak, Triangle, Tail of Rump, AIGUILLETE DE RUMSTEK, AIGUILLETE

Corazón de Cuadril—Eye of Rump, Rump, Cap and Tail Off, NOIX (COUER) DE RUMSTEK

Cuadrada—Bottom Round-Stewing

Cuadril—Rump Roast, Rump Steaks

Entraña—Skirt Steak, Thick Skirt, Hanging Tender, ONGLET, HAMPE

Falda—Flank Steak, Skirt Steak (outer), Navel, OS BALNC

Garrón—Shank, PLAT DE JARRET, POT AU FEU, JARRET ARRIERE

Lomo—Tenderloin, Fillet, FILET

Marucha—Short Ribs, Shoulder Clod, Blade Clod, RAQUERRE, PALERON, PALETTE, MACREUSE, A POT-AU-FAU

Matambre —Plate, Rose Meat

Milanesa—Minute Steak

Nalga—Round Stewing Beef, Topside, COIN, TENDE DETRANCHE

Ojo de Bife—Rib Eye Roast

Osobuco—Osso Busso. The garrón and brazuelo are the boneless versions of the same cut.

Paleta—Shoulder Roast

Palomita†—Butterfly Cut near Shoulder Roast

Peceto—Round Steak, Roast Eye of Round, Round Roll, *TRANCHE, PIECE RONDE, ROTI DE BOEUF*

Pecho—Brisket

Rabo —Oxtail

Ros Bif—Roast Beef. This has no resemblance to the cut of beef used for English roast beef; it refers to cheap stewing beef.

Tapa de Aguja—A special cut sometimes called "Asado de carnicero."

Tapa de Asado†—Rib Cap Roast, *DESSUS DE CÔTES*

Tapa de Cuadril—Cap of Rump Roast

Tapa de Nalga—Cap of Round Roast

Tira de Asado†—Short Ribs

Tortuguita—Round Roast (Knuckle), Heel Beef, *GÎTE, EPAIS DU JANSET*

Vacio—Plate, Flank Steak, *BAVETTE*

Achuras (Offal) Offal meats are used quite frequently in asados.

Chinchulínes—Lower Intestines

Corazón—Heart

Criadillas—Testicles

Hígado—Liver

Lengua—Tongue

Molleja—Sweetbreads, thymus

Riñón—Kidney

Sesos—Brains

Tripa Gorda—Tripe, large intestines

Ubre—Udder

Cuts for The Task Hopefully the below table showing the best cuts for various purposes should prove useful when shopping:

Steaks	BIFE DE LOMO, BIFE DE CHORIZO, BIFE ANGOSTO
Roasts	LOMO, COLITA DE CUADRIL, CORAZÓN DE CUADRIL, PECETO
Stews	CUADRADA, NALGA, BOLA DE LOMO, TORTUGUITA
Grill (Asado)	ASADO, TIRA DE ASADO, VACIO, BIFE DE VACIO, LOMO, BIFES DE LOMO, BIFE DE CHORIZO
Milanesas	MILANESA DE: CUADRIL, LOMO, NALGA, BOLA DE LOMO
Stir fry	CHURRASCO DE CUADRIL

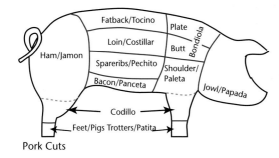

Pork Cuts

Packaged Pork U.S., UK and Argentine pork cuts are very similar. The Argentine cut *"bondiola"* corresponds to the plate and butt in the U.S.. In addition, the ham and shoulder cuts may have an additional cut, the *codillo*, roughly corresponding to a ham shank. If you wish to prepare a fresh ham, you will need to go to a *carniceria* or the meat counter of a large super market such as Jumbo, Norte, or Carrefour. You may have difficulty finding one because of the Argentine preference for cured hams.

Bifes de jamón—thick cuts from a fresh ham
Bondiola—Boston butt
 sin hueso—boneless
Carre—Pork loin
Cerdo flaco—Lean pork
Chorizos—Sausages
Cochinillo—Suckling pig
Costillas de Cerdo—Pork chops

Costillas (Cerdo)—Ribs
Jamón—Ham
Lechón[1]— Suckling pig
Loganiza—Sausage
Lomos de cerdo—Pork tenderloin
Pechito con hueso—Pork spare ribs[2]
Panceta[3]— pork belly
ahumado—smoked (bacon)
Salchicha—sausage
Tocino—back fat
con cuero—rind on

Packaged Lamb U.S., UK and Argentine lamb cuts are also very similar. The major difference is in how the forelegs are cut. The *"paleta"* is cut higher than

1. Cochinillo is younger than lechón.
2. Usually labeled as ribs
3. Panceta is not bacon, so do not expect it to cook as such. It is a good substitute for bacon in many recipes, but you'll need to understand how it behaves.

121

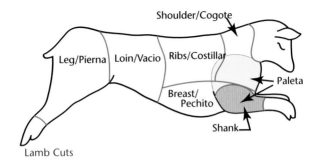

Lamb Cuts

the corresponding U.S. cut, the shank.

"Lamb" is defined to encompass meat of a sheep less than one year old, while mutton is used for the meat of a sheep one year old or older. The term "*lechal*" is used for the youngest lambs, those who are still nursing. Sheep are raised all over the world and sheep growers of each country tout their lamb as having the best flavor. Like its beef, sheep raised in the U.S. is grain-fed for about two and a half months. The practice in Argentina, as well as New Zealand and Australia, is for the sheep to feed naturally upon grass. Within Argentina, Patagonia claims to raise the best lamb because Patagonian sheep feed on such sparse vegetation that they grow slowly and have less fat. However within Buenos Aires markets you will seldom find any mention of the origin of the meat—of course, it will all be from Argentina.

Costillas de Cordero—Lamb chops
gruesas—thick
Pernil de Cordero—Leg of lamb (Hind leg)
Vacio de Cordero—Crown roast of lamb
Paleta de Cordero—Leg of lamb (fore leg), good for shish kebob
Vacio—Loin

Other Meats The following are some other meats that one will encounter while shopping in a *carniceria* or special *granja* store.
Chivito—Goat meat
Ciervo—Venison (Deer meat)
Conejo—Rabbit
Fiambres—Cold cuts
Liebre—Wild rabbit (Hare)
Panchos—Hot dogs
Riñones—Kidneys (usually lamb)

Poultry When you are shopping for poultry products, whether in a supermarket or elsewhere, these are the terms you will encounter.

Pollo—Chicken
Eviserado—gutted
Deshuesado—deboned
Sin menudos—without giblets
Panzas—gizzards
Pechuga—breast
Muslo—thigh
Patas—legs
Codorniz—Quail
Faisán—Pheasant
Gallina—Hen

Gallo—Rooster
Ganso(a)—Gander (goose)
Magret[1] (de pato)—Duck breast
Pavo—Turkey
Pavita—Turkey hen (small)
Pato—Duck
Perdiz—Partridge
Pollitos bebes—Pullets (young chickens)

Fish The following table should help you select a fish for cooking based on the texture and characteristics of the cooked fish.

Fatty, Firm-textured	ANCHOA ATÚN BONITA	CONGRIO PALOMETA
Fatty, Flaky-textured	CABALLA SALMÓN TRUCHA	
Lean, Firm-textured	CAZÓN MERO PEZ ANGEL	PEZ ESPADA RAYA TIBURÓN
Lean, Flaky-textured	ABADEJO BACALAO BESUGO BROTOLA CHERNA CORVINA CORVINA NEGRA LENGUADO MERLUZA	PARGO PEJERREY PESCADILLA POLACA RÓBALO SALMÓN DE MAR SALMONETE SARGO

123

Useful Terms When Dining Out

Are there any...?—¿Hay ...?[1]

I would like ...—Quiero ...

... toothpicks—palillos, escarbadientes

... a knife—un cuchillo

... a fork—un tenedor

... a spoon—una cuchara

... the salt—el sal

... the pepper—la pimienta

... a napkin—una servilleta

... no smoking area—área de no fumadores

The menu (wine list), please—La carta (de vino), por favor.

This is too salty (cold).—Demasiado salado (frió).

The meal was very good.—La comida estuvo excelente.

This (plate. preparation) is delicious.—Esta riquísimo.

Do you accept credit cards?—¿Acepta tarjetas de crédito?

1. If you need something, it is simpler to ask if there are any rather than using the more complex, "I want, I would like" form.

When do you serve meals (breakfast, lunch)?—¿A qué hora se come (desayuna, almuerza)?

We would like a quieter location.—Preferimos un lug no tan ruidoso.

Something is wrong with thi dish.—Hay algo en este plato que no funciona.

This glass is dirty—El vaso es sucio.

This table is unstable.—La m es inestable.

We are in a hurry.—Estamos apurados.

I would like to make a reservation.—Quiero hacer u reserva.

I'd like something less expensive.—Resulta un poco caro./Me parece caro.

What do you recommend?—¿Qué me aconseja?

Can you recommend a local wine?—¿Puede usted recom dar un vino de la región?

We would like to share the salad.—Quisiéramos compa la ensalada.

Conversion of Metric & English Units

1 KILOGRAM (KG)	2.205 POUNDS (LB)
1 POUND (LB)	454 GRAMS (GM)
1 METER (M)	3.281 FEET (FT)
1 FOOT (FT)	0.305 METER (M)
1 LITER (L)	0.220 IMPERIAL GALLONS
	0.264 US GALLONS
	1.759 PINTS
1 IMPERIAL GALLON	4.546 LITER
1 US GALLON	3.785 LITER
1 ACRE	2.471 HECARES
1 SQ. METER	10.7639 SQ. FT.

Oven Temperat

°C	°F
110	225
120	250
140	275
150	300
160	325
180	350
190	375
200	400
220	425
230	450
240	475
250	500

Index

About The Authors

Dereck Foster

Dereck Foster was born in Buenos Aires in 1931 and, except for the period 1953-1959 spent in Spain, South Africa and other countries outside of Argentina, has lived there all of his life. While in Spain, he visited his first winery and his passion for food and wine was born. He has always been a journalist specializing in gastronomy and travel, which has allowed him to visit 36 countries on five continents.

He has been the Buenos Aires Herald's Food and Wine columnist since 1967 and lately its editor. Dereck lectures widely and for eleven years lectured on food and drink at the Salvador university in Buenos Aires.

Richard Tripp

Richard Tripp, or Dick as he is more commonly called, was born in North Carolina in 1940. As an active duty officer in the U.S. Navy, he traveled extensively and continued to do so after his retirement in 1988 when he moved to Brussels with his wife, a member of the U.S. Foreign Service, and other posts in Madrid and Buenos Aires. They now live in El Paso, Texas

Dick became interested in food and cooking when he was young and his interest in wine started to develop in 1967 during four years of duty in Northern California, close to the California wine centers.

Acknowledgements

Cover design by Alissa S. McMahon.

We would like to acknowledge the work of and express our thanks to the following organizations and photographers whose work enhance this book. The other photographs and drawings are those of the authors.

Bodega Finca Flichman 57
Gonzalo Castro 22
Marshall Carter-Tripp 1, 8, 9, 28, 70, 112
Alison Goudreault (two cover inserts)
Roberto Sanz 31, 55, 56, 76, 82, 114
Divina Minkévich 25, 30, 32, 42, 43, 49, 54, 59, 62, 69

We would also like to express our heartfelt thanks to the following folks for the permission to use their recipes:

"Betty" Nauta, Estancia Telken 104
Alberto Vazquez-Prego 105, 106, 107, 109, 110, 111
Florencia Perkins, Bodega "La Rosa," Michel Torino Hnos. 108

Notes